THE COMMUNION SABBATH.

THE

COMMUNION SABBATH.

BY

NEHEMIAH ADAMS, D. D.,
PASTOR OF ESSEX STREET CHURCH, BOSTON.

THIRD EDITION.

BOSTON:
S. K. WHIPPLE AND COMPANY,
161 WASHINGTON STREET.
1857.

CAMBRIDGE:
ALLEN AND FARNHAM, STEREOTYPERS AND PRINTERS.

INTRODUCTORY NOTE.

VIEWING with deep interest, from time to time, those who leave the House of Worship when the Lord's Supper is to be administered, the thought has presented itself of preparing a volume which might, in some parts of it, be interesting as well as useful to them.

While, therefore, this book is also designed for Communicants, they to whom it owes its origin are kept in mind.

And while the book, as a Communicant's companion, does not follow the useful, ordinary method of a series of questions addressed to the communicant, it is hoped and believed that it will no less lead him to examine himself, and so to eat of that bread and drink of that cup.

CONTENTS.

I.

CHRIST DIED FOR US.

"BUT GOD COMMENDETH HIS LOVE TOWARD US, IN THAT, WHILE WE WERE YET SINNERS, CHRIST DIED FOR US."

WE would sooner do and suffer any thing for others than die for them. When men, in their love and compassion for others, find that they are likely to perish themselves, they generally stop, then flee from the burning room, or shake off the drowning man, who by his grasp would prevent them from saving their own lives. Parents, husbands, wives, sometimes throw themselves into the arms of death impulsively, when they see a child or companion perishing, but a deliberate surrender of one's self to die to save another, is extremely rare. A man who is merely without reproach, a negative character, one with nothing strikingly good about him, can hardly awaken interest enough in others to die for him deliberately, leaving out of view sudden, impulsive acts of heroism. Scarcely for a righteous man would one die, yet, peradventure, for a man with something positively interesting about him, for a good man, some would even dare to die. Still it is a rare case. Men would say, I have a family, or, I am under obligations to others. If the best and most useful man were ready to die, and the question were asked, Who will die and save his life? which of us would be persuaded to make the substitution? If, weary of the world, one should consent, his motive would prevent his act from being an exception to what has now been said.

That we may see in what light we regard the substitution of one life for other lives, we will imagine the following case.

A crew, escaped from a wreck on the high seas, have filled their boat to the water's edge, and occupied every possible place in it. Another survivor of the wreck swims up, boldly lays hold of the stern, and begs to be taken in. This unhappy being is yourself. With streaming eyes and voices choked with grief, they say, There is no room for you. Benumbed with holding on, you perceive that soon you must resign yourself to a watery grave. Then the sorrows of death compass you, and the pains of hell get hold upon you. One of the company feels unutterable compassion, and says to the rest, He shall take my place. What reason does he give? That man, he says, I have reason to believe, is not prepared to die. My peace is made with God. If I save him from death, it may subdue him to repentance, and save his soul. The company refusing to take any responsibility in the case, the man leaps into the sea. He is irrecoverably gone. His place being vacant, you are drawn out of the sea, placed in his seat, and reach your home.

That man died for you. He bid farewell to all which was dear to him; in full health and strength he met the anguish of dying, gave up his body without a burial to be devoured in the deep, or wander in the currents of the ocean, or bleach on a strange shore. He chose to appear before his God, his probation terminated, to meet his unalterable doom. We will raise no question about the right of an individual thus to sacrifice his life. We are concerned now only with his act and his motive. His motive was purely benevolent. He saved your life to save your soul. You were a stranger to him till you sailed together, and he was under no obligations to you of any kind.

As you sat in your peaceful home, or lay on your bed, and oftentimes in your journeys, in your business, in all companies, the memory of that friend would affect you deeply. At the evening lamp, or in the night watches, as the blast pressed against your window, and your thoughts were directed to the sea and its perils, you would remember, A man died for me. The cup of suffering he took from my hand, and drank it himself. He pressed his way before me, and met the king of terrors, and turned the monster from me. I live by his death. All that I have is due to his love; it has been the means of my conversion to God; my eternity in heaven, under God, I owe to him.

What may we suppose you would do to signify your gratitude? Could you learn that there were relatives of his to whom you could show kindness, you would find it a relief to your feelings if you might help them. The family name of the man, wherever you should meet it, would always thrill you. When the anniversary of your rescue came round, no day in the year would bring with it such thoughts and feelings. Evermore this would be the impression upon your mind, A man died for me. To the grave of the ocean he voluntarily and deliberately went down, and saved me from death and hell.

How would it be if others with you were saved by this man? Would that lessen your love, and sense of obligation? Let us consider whether it would be so.

The boat, containing yourself and the whole of the crew, we will now suppose, was accidentally left fastened to the wreck. The end of the rope which is in the boat cannot by any means be severed; the wreck is settling and will soon go down, carrying with it all your company; they see that the end of the rope attached to the wreck can be cast off, but cannot be reached by the arm alone; some one must lift an instrument and push it off; the wind is blowing a gale, from the wreck; you have no oars, and the man who should push the rope from its fastening into the water must give up all expectation of returning to the boat, and will see it drift away, leaving him to die. Could he grasp the rope as it falls, he would be saved; but this is impossible. Time is wasting; the wreck gives signs of sinking, when one of the company says, I will give my life for you all. He refuses the proposal to cast lots, — he cannot be restrained; and then, with an unutterable struggle of feeling on your part, you let him make the sacrifice. As he shakes hands with you severally, and that word, farewell, comes from you each in turn and all together, confused with loud weeping, do you think that this mean thought would rise in your mind: After all, I am indebted to him only my proportional share with the rest? No; if you had the heart of a human being, you would embrace him, saying, O my brother, will you die for me? The work is done, and as you drift away from him, leaving him on his coffin of a wreck, waving with his hand his farewell, and you finally see him engulfed and disappear, say, would you be willing to give up any part of your obligation, that it might be borne by another? Your constant declaration would be, He died for me.

All that has now been imagined has, for substance, but in an infinitely higher sense, been done for each of us.

Many think of Christ, and of their obligations to him, as they do, for example, of the services rendered by the patriots of their country to the whole people, but do not think of him as bestowing favor on them in particular, or expressly for each of them. This is erroneous, for it is the excellent glory and praise of Christ as a Saviour, that he is to every individual all which he can be to the race, and that every one can with as perfect truth appropriate his whole redeeming work, his birth, his sufferings, his death, his intercession, as though he alone were to be saved by Christ.

We admit that he died for all. "Behold the Lamb of God which taketh away the sin of the world." These words, not to quote others like them, teach us that one human being is at least as much included in the benefits intended by the Saviour's death as another. God is no less the creator of each of us in being the parent of the whole human family.

But the death of Christ is indispensably necessary for our individual salvation. Repentance is a personal thing, so is faith; and the Saviour with his whole atoning work is as necessary to save one soul as the souls of a race. For the same principle of Divine government would be violated in saving one soul without an atonement, as in saving all; and the converse is true, to save one soul involves the whole great principle of atonement. Were any one of us the only sinner of the race, to save him without a sacrifice for sin would as truly violate the rule of justice as to save a world. A case at law involving a very small sum, may call up the fundamental questions of jurisprudence.

Christ himself, it may be noticed, very frequently speaks in the singular number when he refers to the salvation of men. "Him that cometh unto me I will in nowise cast out." "And I will raise him up at the last day." "Behold, I stand at the door and knock; if any man hear my voice and open the door, I will come in unto him and sup with him, and he with me." "If a man love me, he will keep my words; and my Father will love him, and we will come unto him, and make our abode with him." This regard for the individual is strikingly shown when the seventy returned with joy, and said that even the devils were subject unto them in the Saviour's name. The Saviour entered into their feelings: "I beheld Satan as lightning fall from heaven." He proceeded to give them further dominion over the powers of evil. But he concludes by saying, "Notwithstanding, in this rejoice not, that the spirits are subject unto you, but rather rejoice because your names are written in heaven." Neither associated privileges and honors, nor official greatness and success, he seems to say, are to be compared with the relation of the individual soul to God.

Repentance and faith are strictly personal. Moreover, each soul needs the whole of Christ and his sacrifice as the ground of justification. Had Christ died for one lost soul, he would not be its Saviour in any other degree than he must now be to each of us if we are saved. If justified at the bar of God, it will be because it can be demanded on behalf of each, "Who is he that condemneth? It is Christ that died."

Indeed, Christ bestows his benefits as a personal Saviour and friend. When a man sees himself to be a sinner, and the bitter cry is wrung from him, "Have mercy upon me, O God," when he sees that he ought to be punished, and wonders at Divine forbearance, it is not enough for him that Christ died for men in general; he seeks a personal interest in Christ, and his effort is to persuade himself that this can be attained. Perhaps there is no such joy and satisfaction known to the human breast as this confidence, Christ is my Saviour, making us say with Thomas, "My Lord and my God." In the extremity of life, there is a face of a friend, a hand, which the dying man cannot spare a moment from his side. We need then the most intimate personal love and kindness. Thus the dying think of Christ and of their personal relation to him, however they may have slighted and forgotten him in life and health. It was so with Voltaire, and Hume, and Paine, who each made personal address to Christ in the agony of dying. The whole may be summed up in these most encouraging words of Jesus, "And this is the will of him that sent me, that every one which seeth the Son, and believeth on him, may have everlasting life; and I will raise him up at the last day." If on that day, an angel should challenge our personal right of admission to heaven, we should rest it on this, Christ died for me, in every sense in which he died for the world, and is as truly my Redeemer through faith in him as he is the Saviour of the world.

Come, then, my soul, if this be true, and if the persuasion is taking possession of you that you have in Christ a personal Saviour, who as truly died for you as though you were the only object of his death, come, and let us look upon him as he lays down his life for you. If he died for you, all which was necessary to accomplish his death was for you. He is coming out of the gate of Jerusalem, bearing a burden on his shoulder; it has the form of a cross, it is a gibbet, it is his dying bed. He cannot lift and bear it any longer; his strength is gone; they change it to the shoulder of another man. I thank thee, Simon; that is for me. The cross is extended on the earth; his form is stretched upon it, I hear the blow of the hammer as each hand and the feet are nailed to the wood; this is for me. They have lifted up the Son of man, for me. Behold, they mock him, and in many ways insult him, and he bears it patiently, for me. It were enough to die for me in a peaceful chamber; the king of terrors is terrible enough in the quiet room with sympathizing friends about the bed. What a dying bed is the cross, with fiends about it in human shape! all this was for me. The sun grows dark, the earth quakes, the rocks rend, the graves open, the dead arise, the vail of the distant temple is rent in sunder without hands, and, "it is finished," — my redemption.

"And was the ransom paid? It was; and paid,
(What can exalt its bounty more!) — for thee."

As though I had taken a lamb from my flock and offered it in sacrifice for my sins, so has Jesus died for me. For this he came from heaven; for this he was God manifest in the flesh; for this he expired, to save me. The last thing which men will do, or can do, for another, Jesus has done for me, and now, if not deceived, I am going to heaven to claim that for no one, nor for the world, did Jesus die more truly than for me. Ye multitude which no man can number, I hear your great anthem; praise him as you will; I am coming, a chief sinner, yet obscure, and less than the least of saints, to take your mighty praise, offer it to Christ, and tell him that you have not expressed one half of my obligations to him, and that his love to me "can ne'er be told." I will take Abel's hymn of praise, the first ascription to redeeming love in heaven, and with all its accumulated strength of love and joy, I will offer it merely as the pitch of my song, and tell my Saviour, as I fail and faint beneath the praise, that "his love can ne'er be told." Does a distant, new world, ages hence, desire to see a redeemed sinner, an object of the Saviour's love, one who owes as much as any other to that love? Here am I, send me. At a period so remote that figures convey no intelligible idea of it, is it asked whether it be true, as frequently expressed on earth, that the redemption of one immortal soul, taking into view its boundless capacity of joy and suffering, were itself enough to warrant all that Christ did and suffered? Every one who reads these lines would then be as eligible as any other to be offered in proof of this momentous truth.

The personal relation and obligation of each soul to Christ, when fully admitted, has great power to give individuality and strength of character to piety, which loses much when we lose ourselves in the great multitude. Moreover, instead of making us exclusive or solitary in our religious feelings, it is sure to expand our love for all men when one feels how Christ has loved him and died for him, and then that every other human being is as truly the object of the Saviour's sufferings and death as he. Toward every one for whom Christ has done all which he has done for him, a Christian feels, at times, great love and desire, and has no rest till every one knows and feels the love which Christ has for him.

When, therefore, the bread is given into my hand, and it is said, Take, eat; this is my body which is broken for you, and, with like assurance, the cup is placed at my lips, let no thought of those around me, nor of the world at large, divide the sufferings of Christ between them and me, but let me cleave to this truth, that he is my personal Saviour. Let me hold converse with him in this persuasion; have covenant transactions with him, and regard him as though he were a private benefactor, who, having sacrificed himself for me, had been restored to life. What inseparable union would I feel to a fellow being, in such circumstances. Then, what a foundation there is for love and attachment between me and Christ, greater already on his part than it can ever be on mine, and drawing me to constant communion and perfect consecration.

The simple object of the Supper is, Remembrance of him, promoted by symbols of his death. I go there to meet him, and to speak with him of his decease which he accomplished at Jerusalem. I shall not hear his voice, nor see his shape, nor do I expect impressions to be made on my mind of his sensible presence; yet there will not be a word in my tongue, nor a thought in my heart, "but lo, O Lord, thou knowest it altogether." Believing him to be at my side, I shall tell him every thing which interests me, ask counsel, lay in his hands all that concerns me for the time to come, and, without seeking a response from him, feel that he has heard, that he fully understands, and will consider it, and in his own time and manner will do for me all that I need. I will recount to him my sins, all the circumstances of them, all their aggravations, and feel it a relief that when my heart condemns me, He is greater than my heart and knoweth all things. I will be sure to speak to him of his mercies, the peculiar features of each blessing, how considerate, how forbearing, how delicate, how generous, how touching, how perfectly suited to my wishes. Anticipating events of deep importance, I will say, If thy presence go not with me, carry me not up hence. No response, did I say, is to be looked for? As I sit and speak to him and weep at his side, there comes a gift, and this message, from him: "This is my body which is broken for you; this cup is the New Testament in my blood which is shed for you." I ask no more. Let him say no more, for how shall he not, with this, also freely give me all things?

If you, reader, are one who leaves the Saviour and his table behind you, know that Christ suffered nothing for another more than he did for you. As you go home, he will walk by your side; as you sit and think of the scene which you have left behind, he will sit with you; and if you choose to be forgetful and use means to banish serious thoughts from your mind, still remember this, There is no one at that table who is more properly there than you would be, no one for whom Christ died more than for you, and there is no one who has been or can be more welcome. Wherever you go, Christ died for you. Whatever you do, Christ died for you. If you are saved, Christ died for you. If you are lost, Christ died for you. How long will you turn away from that table which infinite love has spread for no human being more truly than for you?

II.

ONE SACRIFICE FOR SINS.

"BUT THIS MAN AFTER HE HAD OFFERED ONE SACRIFICE FOR SINS, FOREVER SAT DOWN ON THE RIGHT HAND OF GOD."

IT was ordained from the beginning that life must be paid for sin. This was the reason for appointing the blood of victims as the emblem of atonement. While there is no value in the blood of animals, as there is in their skins and flesh, the Scripture says, The life is in the blood, and the appointment of blood, therefore, to make atonement, signified that life must be paid for sin.

It would seem that men would have sinned but seldom, knowing what they must do to atone for it. Having trespassed against God, and being penitent on account of it, something yet remains for the sinner to do. He goes to his flock and takes a lamb or goat, or to his herds and selects a young bullock, binds him, and brings him to the priest. As he passes along, the soul of the sinner is melted within him. This animal, he says, is not to die in order to feed me and mine; its innocent head is to bear my sin; the knife will demand its blood because I have done wrong. A creature about to be sacrificed must have excited strong emotions in one who, for his own sin, was leading the innocent victim to be put to death. The victim was required to be the best of its kind, without blemish, and was therefore in itself an interesting object. Its fear, its struggles, its blood, its moan, its eye fixed in death, one might suppose, would prevent the repetition of a sin, and restrain from other transgressions; for the thought, If I sin, one must die for me, a life must go for my life, would have the effect, if any thing could do it, to keep one back from presumptuous sins. Any thing but sin could be prevented by such considerations, and any thing but the heart which is desperately wicked would yield to such a motive.

In addition to special and private sacrifices for sins, there was a yearly day of atonement, when the high-priest, with imposing ceremonies, entered alone into the holy of holies, not without blood, which he offered for himself and for the errors of the people. Thus for four thousand years the animal tribes, by their appointed representatives, paid for man the forfeiture of his life by their own. For thousands of years the priests of God stood daily offering the same sacrifices, with their impressive ordinances of the scape-goat, the living bird dipped in its fellow's blood and set free, the running brook, the ashes of an heifer, and the sprinkling of the book of the law with blood, all holding forth the same truths, The wages of sin is death; and, Without shedding of blood, is no remission.

But we are told that there is no inherent value or efficacy in the death of a bullock, or lamb, or bird, to atone for sin. Expressly does the Scripture assert this: "It is impossible that the blood of bulls and of goats should take away sin." What satisfaction, or recompence, for the moral turpitude of stealing, or lying, or uncleanness, could it be, to offer up an animal to death? Does the price of a bullock express the amount of guilt in any sin? Or, if sin, as we are taught, makes the sinner deserving of eternal death, is the life of an animal any proper substitution for the death of the soul?

Nothing is more clearly, and in a more forcible and impressive manner, revealed in Scripture than this: The sufferings and death of Christ, prefigured by ancient sacrifices, are an atonement for sin. Those sacrifices, we are informed, meant Christ, they pointed to Christ. A question is frequently raised here, Whether the people had any proper knowledge of Christ, or so much as a distinct reference to him and his sufferings, in their sacrifices? The belief that they had no such reference, prevents some from viewing the ancient sacrifices as types of Christ, or the sufferings and death of Christ as having any real connection with them; and the comparison of them to those sacrifices is taken as allegorical.

There is an illustration of the truth on this point, which, if properly guarded, and understood with limitations, will help us to resolve this difficulty. The objection is, that the mass of the people, probably, had no proper knowledge of Christ, nor any distinct reference to him, in their sacrifices for sin. For the sake of the argument, we will at present admit this to have been so.

The paper of a bank-note is not worth a dollar, though it is engraved, and signed by the proper authorities. In itself, that paper, offered in place of money, on the ground of intrinsic value in the paper, would be absurd. But there is an agreed value conferred on that paper, and established by law, so that the thing which in itself, we may say, is worthless, may, by appointment of law, be worth the real coin which it represents.

And now let it be considered how few of those into whose hands that paper passes, understand, while fewer still recall to mind, the idea of paper currency, as a legal representative of specie. Give it to a child, a laborer, perhaps we may say to any one whom you may happen to meet, and while not one in a thousand would consider that it has no intrinsic value, but is only a representative of the precious metals, not one in ten thousand of those who do know it, would, at the moment of using the note, refer in his thoughts to this specie basis. Still, it would be wholly wrong to say of any community, The idea of a metallic basis to its circulating medium is not understood, is not believed; for the doctrine is established, is known and acted upon, and the presence of this paper is evidence of it, though the popular mind does not recognize it in its current acts. So that we may without difficulty believe that the use of sacrifices answered every purpose as an atonement for sin, even if the people did not, generally, refer in their thoughts to that great appointment of God which gave them their acceptance. Illustrations occur on every hand of acts indispensable to comfort and life which are unaccompanied by a proper knowledge of the reasons for them. For example, not one in a hundred who use a pump know any thing of the valves in it, much less think of the lower box, which they never feel nor see, and of whose operation there is to them no evidence whatever.

But there is a passage in that wonderful book, the Epistle to the Hebrews, which places it beyond doubt that the people understood the incomplete and prophetic nature of their sacrifices: "The Holy Ghost this signifying, that the way into the holiest of all was not yet made manifest, while as the first tabernacle was yet standing, which was a figure for the time then present,—that could not make him that did the service perfect as pertaining to the conscience; which stood only in—carnal ordinances, imposed on them until the time of reformation." Here we see that the "conscience" of a sinner felt the need of something beyond his victim to atone for his sin.

The doctrine of a suffering Messiah was known in those days. Christ said to the Jews, "Your father Abraham rejoiced to see my day; and he saw it and was glad." Moreover, we read, "And the Scripture, foreseeing that God would justify the heathen by faith, preached before the Gospel unto Abraham." Christ and his Gospel were therefore known to Abraham, and by tradition such important knowledge was, of course, preserved, from age to age. But still it is true that, in accordance with the divine plan of progressive revelation, the doctrine of Christ's righteousness and of salvation by his death, "was not made known unto the sons of men as it was revealed unto his holy apostles and prophets by the Spirit;" but sacrifices for sins were appointed and used as the acceptable way of approach to God. Worthless in themselves, wholly inadequate to atone for guilt, they were agreed upon to represent the infinite sacrifice which once, in the end of the world, Christ was to make, when he should put away sin by the offering up of himself. The ancient worshipper who came to make atonement for his sin, was warranted in relying on the blood of his slain bullock, or goat, for the pardon of his sin, as we are in relying upon a thing which has no substantive value, yet is agreed upon as an equivalent.

But the time came when all these oblations were to pass away, and we hear One, in the greatness of his strength, proclaim, "Sacrifice and offering, and burnt offerings and offering for sin, thou wouldest not, neither hadst pleasure therein; which are offered by the law. Then said he, Lo, I come—to do thy will, O God. By the which will, we are sanctified through the offering of the body of Jesus Christ once for all."

He, by his sufferings and death, did that which all the beasts and the altars professed to do, but which without his appointed sacrifice would have been impossible.

The writer of the Epistle to the Hebrews labors, with the closest logic and singular power, to show, not that Christ was a King, nor a Prophet, both of which he is elsewhere proved to be, but a High-Priest. Now a high-priest, as his readers well knew, had, for his specific duty, which distinguished his office from that of other men, to offer gifts and sacrifices for sin. Observe his statement and reasoning: "We have such an High-Priest, who is set on the right hand of the throne of the majesty in the heavens. For every high-priest is ordained to offer gifts and sacrifices; wherefore it is of necessity that this man have somewhat also to offer." This, we all feel, is sound reasoning, and the question naturally arises, what offering had he? The answer is, he "needeth not daily, as those high-priests, to offer up sacrifice, first for his own sins, and then for the people's; for this he did once, when he offered up himself." "Neither by the blood of goats and calves, but by his own blood, he entered in once into the holy place, having obtained eternal redemption for us." "He is the Mediator of the New Testament — by means of death for the redemption of the transgressions that were under the first testament," thus giving sanction and efficacy to all the ancient sacrifices. It was not necessary that he should "offer himself often, as the high-priest entered into the holy place every year with blood of others, for then must he often have suffered since the foundation of the world; but now once, in the end of the world, hath he appeared, to put away sin by the sacrifice of himself." "So Christ was once offered to bear the sins of many."

What has become of all those high-priests and altars, bullocks and rams, the scape-goat and ashes of an heifer, the bird dipped in his fellow's blood and set free? Have we no sins? Has the world become perfect? Or, has the character of God changed? Does he forgive sins now without any reference to sacrifice of any kind? Is Christ as a teacher, the fulfilment of all those offerings for sin?

In words as plain as possible, Jesus Christ is declared to be a substitute for all those offerings for sin by the offering up of himself to suffer and die. In order to this, he says, "A body hast thou prepared me." His forerunner announces him to the world, but by what name? "Behold the Lamb of God which taketh away the sin of the world." The prophets dwell upon his sufferings and death, and he himself, expounding their prophecies after his resurrection, said, "Ought not Christ to suffer these things, and to enter into his glory?" So we are told that "this man after he had offered one sacrifice for sins, forever sat down on the right hand of God."

He who was in the beginning, the Word, who "was with God and was God, the same was in the beginning with God," became flesh, and suffered and died, his divine nature giving worth and efficacy to his sufferings and death, which were appointed to do that which his representatives, the ancient sacrifices, professed to do in his stead, until he should come, which is, to atone for sin.

We must endeavor to make this real and clear to our minds, that he who was laid in the manger, and suffered on the cross, and slept in the tomb, and ascended to heaven, is, to the whole race of man, and to every individual of the race, that which the ancient sacrifices were to the people who offered them; that he takes the place and fulfils the meaning of the lamb on the day of atonement, the goat and the scape-goat, the one bleeding, and the other bearing away the sins of the people, the bird whose blood was shed upon his fellow setting him free. Reading the Psalms and Prophets, and the New Testament, with this in view, their phraseology is not only intelligible, but comes with overwhelming force, and there is no way to evade it but either to turn it all into allegory, or to reject it and the book that contains it as contrary to reason. To make it an allegory is to receive the ancient sacrifices as the substantial verities, and to regard Christ and his work as merely compared with them in figurative forms of speech, to catch the attention and please the fancy of Jews. Christ is no such secondary object. He is the building and they the scaffolding; Christ is not their shadow; they were a shadow thrown from him, four thousand years previous to his coming; and, as a shadow, they, of course, gave a proper idea of him and his office. Had he been coming merely as a teacher, or as an example, or as a messenger to declare the mind of God more perfectly, the shadow which he threw before him was surely most unapt, for the impression made by those rites was, God requires propitiatory sacrifice for sin; God cannot be approached by a sinner except by mediators, offering life to expiate guilt. That Jesus Christ himself by his life and death enforced these truths as the principal object of his coming into the world, is obvious from the impression which the whole world of readers, with so few exceptions, have received. To set it aside as contrary to our idea of what is suitable and proper, is surely to claim a province for human reason between which and the assumption of divine authority, there hardly remains so much as a single step. Whether sin is an evil, and how great an evil, whether it can be forgiven, and in what way, and on what conditions, are questions which God himself must answer; and being answered, our province is to judge of the evidence that they are answered, but not to question their propriety. As to the divinely appointed method of forgiving sin, we can no more sit in judgment upon it, than we could object to the different number of moons in the firmaments of different planets.

Great violence is done to language, and to the general tenor of Scripture, and to our moral faculties, by converting plain and literal representations of the Saviour's atoning sufferings and death into metaphor, as the hot sands of a desert change rain into mirage. A principle of interpretation is then adopted which makes it easy to break the force, or turn the point, of every revealed truth, and God has no longer any moral influence over our minds. Happy they who are kept, or have been recovered, from such a state of mind, and who receive the language of heavenly worship, for example, in its literal sense, with all its rapture of gratitude and love: "Thou art worthy, for thou wast slain and hast redeemed us to God by thy blood out of every kindred and tongue and people and nation."

Let us look with a glance at the hundreds of millions of Europe, Asia, Africa, America, and Oceanica, and think, that not one of these can reach heaven except as, in some way, a debtor to His sufferings and death, or to the principles of divine government as affected by Him, who is said to have been "slain from the foundation of the world."

The redeemed who were seen in vision to be a multitude which no man can number, are each of them in heaven through his blood. To every one of us, this Lamb of God stands in the relation of a sacrifice for sins, his Passover lamb, his substitute, by sufferings and death, as the victim of divine justice, the ground of his plea for pardon, the reason why God can forgive him, his ransom, his Redeemer, the propitiation for his sins.

Is there a being who stands in such a relation as this to me? is there one whose office, whose name is, Lamb of God, which taketh away the sin of the world? is he, to me alone, all and every thing which he is to the whole world? If so, nothing concerns me so much as to understand it. What does it mean? What does it imply?

On my way to the house of God, a great company of my friends, my best friends, intelligent, sober-minded men, come with haste and earnestness around me, and fill me with astonishment and wonder at their coming. What has happened? Do you know, they say, what we have been doing in your behalf? There is a company of men seeking your life; we have succeeded in giving bonds for you, and you are for the present at liberty. What have I done? These friends are not beside themselves. What is my offence? How am I in danger?

Suppose that I had lived two thousand years ago, in Judæa. I am met in the same way by a company of esteemed men. We have been, they say, to the high-priest on your behalf, each with a bullock or ram, or lamb; a hundred victims have bled to expiate your sin. What sin? But the character of these friends places it beyond a doubt that they, at least, believe me to be involved in some terrible guilt and danger.

There is one on the throne of heaven, God manifest in the flesh, worshipped by all the heavenly hosts, swaying the sceptre of universal empire, who once upon a cross on Mount Calvary, died for me. Yes, for me. Not merely for my sins as the part of a great whole, but for my sins, so that I cannot be saved except by the personal application to me of his sufferings and death. Finding this asserted and established in the Word of God, I can have no rest till I receive it and act upon it as the most important truth which God has ever revealed to me. Nothing, surely, can affect me so much as this. Were I a state prisoner, and from the window of my cell should see casks of gold brought into the prison yard, and piled up till the sum reached to millions, the feeling would be, What worth, what importance, attaches to me, that my government must redeem me even at this price?

O, my soul, you were "not redeemed with corruptible things as silver and gold, but with the precious blood of Christ as of a lamb without blemish and without spot." You are "bought with a price." One was made sin for me, who knew no sin. He was wounded for my transgressions, bruised for my iniquities, the chastisement of my peace was upon him, and by his stripes I am healed. The worth of my soul, my guilt, my danger, are here set forth as they could be in no other way. I may have made light of sin. I may not have felt that I am a sinner. I may not have been sorry for my sin. I may not have made it my first endeavor to be delivered from that, and to abstain from that, which here appears to be of such moment. Henceforth, Christ and his sacrifice for sins must be the great consideration with me, moving me to view myself as God has viewed me, as a sinner to an extent and with liabilities which God has estimated as needing such a work as that of Christ to atone for; as a debtor to infinite love, as not my own, but bought with a price, as under obligations to persuade each fellow-creature of his danger and of his remedy, the same in every respect as mine.

Let him who complains that he has never been able to view himself as a sinner in any proper degree, begin with this truth, that Christ "bare our sins in his own body on the tree," that "God hath laid on him the iniquity of us all," that "we shall be saved from wrath through him;" let him dwell upon this truth till he sees his danger, and his refuge too. It is best to begin with Christ in every endeavor to affect our minds upon any religious subject, nor can one who believes the Scripture in its representations concerning Christ and him crucified, and truly desires to know what is implied in his death for sin, fail to obtain a proper knowledge of himself, and of the way to be saved.

Perhaps we are conscious of sin, and are persuaded that our condemnation is just.

Let us suppose, then, that one should see a great inclosure filled with animals, as far as the eye can reach, and while he surveys them, the air over his head is darkened by an immense flight of birds, prolonged for many hours, and he is told, All these God has appointed and provided as a sacrifice for your sins; justice requires a substitute for your punishment, and is satisfied upon your repentance, and acceptance of this sacrifice, with this substitution.

More, infinitely more than this, God has done for me. If the altars of the world for four thousand years had burned for me, with their countless victims, the sacrifice which has been made for my soul exceeds them. There is a striking omission of all epithets, as though even inspired language had none adequate to the occasion, when it is said, "Ye are bought with — a price." If Christ died for me, there is no reason why I may not be forgiven. If the whole world should, in the same hour, ask for pardon through his death, his death is an atonement sufficient for all the world. Surely, then, "he is able to save them to the uttermost who come unto God by him."

Such are the truths, and such the wondrous things,

implied, when we show forth the Lord's death. The celebration of the Lord's Supper, therefore, is a solemnity which has no parallel, and never had one, and, in this world, it never can be equalled. With every successive approach to it, we will endeavor to enter more fully into the meaning of it, and, in order to this, live more habitually, during the intervals of our communion seasons, under the influence of this stupendous sacrifice for sins.

Believing, as the Scripture tells us, that this sacrifice is finished, and that this priest needeth not daily to offer for sins, because he did this once, when he offered himself, we look with interest and concern upon many of our fellow men who make repetitions of the Saviour's sacrifice. With strong desire to free them from these needless ceremonies, we should persuade them that it is as wrong to add any thing to the Saviour's one sacrifice for sins as to take any thing from it; that human victims might as well be crucified, to set forth Christ and his sacrifice, as to do any thing more with the bread and wine than to eat it and drink it, in remembrance of him. We cannot be sufficiently grateful for the simplicity which is in Christ, so strikingly set forth in the Lord's Supper. The senses are appealed to, their aid is not refused, but is employed, in spiritual things, yet in the most simple manner.

"As often as ye do eat this bread and drink this cup, ye do show the Lord's death till he come." Such is the employment of that company of Christians to be gathered to-day around the Lord's table; — they show the Lord's death, the greatest event, and, to each of us, the most important event, and in its influence upon the whole race of man, an event involving the greatest consequences, of any thing which, to our knowledge, has ever transpired. Yes it is a great thing to have a place at that table, to be looked upon by heaven as a participator in that transaction, being personally concerned in the benefits which flow from that one sacrifice which is there set forth.

We, as it were, show the Lord's death to divine justice, as the ground of our justification.

We show it to ourselves as the all-sufficient reason why we may look for pardon; as the memorial of infinite love for our souls, and as the constraining motive to live not unto ourselves.

We show it to the congregation who assemble with us; we cause that table to be spread, we appoint due solemnities in our approach to it, we separate ourselves to receive the ordinance, and thus we perpetually remind the world around us of the one sacrifice for them and for us. There is no transaction in which men are statedly engaged, which will hereafter seem to us, as we look back to earth, more important and more solemn than the ordinance which commemorated the sacrifice for sins.

The Communion Sabbath may properly remind us

of the day of atonement, when the high-priest entered alone once a year, into the holy of holies, to make reconciliation for the sins of the people. Though we offer up no sacrifice, we commemorate the sacrifice of Christ for the world, and we call attention to it. There is a high-priest appearing with a sacrifice for each of us, and he himself has appointed the Supper to remind us of it. We cannot with safety, nor can we innocently, be indifferent to this appointment, nor, if we have a proper sense of our most affecting obligations, can we fail to attend upon this ordinance with self-examination, with grateful love, and with practical application of the truths involved in it to our characters and lives.

But, in a passage which has now been frequently quoted, in this connection, there occurs a word which calls forth the question, Is it possible that one who stands in such a relation, as we have now considered, to this great High-Priest, can be at present, or can hereafter be regarded and treated, as his enemy? An Israelite, we may suppose, would feel nothing but reverential love toward his high-priest making intercession for him, though merely with the blood of others. How must it have been had the high-priest gone within the vail to die for him? Had one been an enemy to him, could he have remained an enemy? "But this man, when he had offered one sacrifice for sin, forever sat down on the right hand of God, from henceforth expecting till his enemies be made his footstool." Can our great

High-Priest, our atoning Saviour and Friend, have, among those for whom he died and intercedes, one who does not love him, one who is indifferent to him, and even an enemy? From the passage just quoted, we learn that he can. "Lord, is it I?"

III.

MIRACLES AT THE CRUCIFIXION.

I. DARKNESS.

"NOW FROM THE SIXTH HOUR THERE WAS DARKNESS OVER ALL THE LAND UNTO THE NINTH HOUR."

AN eclipse of the sun could not have happened at that season, it being the time of the Jewish passover, which occurred at the full of the moon. Moreover, a total eclipse of the sun, as we call it, does not continue, like this darkness, for three hours. It was preternatural, and, like the other remarkable events in nature at the time, was appointed as a solemnity of the crucifixion.

It was suitable that the heavens should be in mourning at the death of the Son of God. He made the heavens and their hosts; "all things were made by him, and without him was not any thing made that was made." Now that he hangs upon a cross, an offering for sin, numbered with the transgressors, well may nature sympathize. Grief in every form in which it could be expressed, was suitable at such a time. The scene at Calvary brought forcibly to mind the ruin and condemnation of man, who was under the wrath of God for sin, the history of the fall and its direful consequences, and the necessity for an infinite sacrifice. God alone was able to expiate the sin of his creatures, by taking man's nature into union with the Divine, in the person of the Word, and making satisfaction to justice by that which He saw to be equivalent, in effect, to the endless punishment of the race. This dread transaction was proceeding; silence and darkness were proper accompaniments; light and joy would not have been appropriate in the death scene of the Son of God. The chamber of death, the house of mourning, invite the shadows rather than the beams of the sun; light is intrusive at such a time; mourning, lamentation, and woe, require the secrecy, and all the influences, of retirement, and that part of the earth was therefore made a chamber of death, with the curtains of darkness hung about it.

It was also appropriate to the condition and feelings of the people of God on earth. It was the time of their apparent defeat. Christ said to the wicked who came to take him, " This is your hour and the power of darkness." The followers of Christ were confounded, and of his immediate disciples, all but one were secreted at home, or were out of sight of danger. That one stood by the cross, hoping against hope, an evening star, which a black cloud at sundown quenches for a night. Is this He that should have delivered Israel? this expiring victim in the hands of murderers? All who loved him and trusted in Him might well put on sackcloth, as the heavens did, for their sun had indeed gone down, and they knew not what should be on the morrow.

Had there been any witnesses of that scene who exercised full faith that Christ would finally triumph, that this humiliation and suffering were only a preparation for victory, even they could not fail to be in heaviness. To the minds of any who saw in Christ the Lamb of God which taketh away the sin of the world, the sufferings of the Saviour must have been the occasion of inexpressible grief. There was something in the sight of Christ which subdued the penitent woman who stood and wept behind him, as he sat at meat. If she were thus affected, Mary Magdalene, and all true penitents, must have wept greatly when Jesus suffered on the tree. The darkened heavens and earth were in sympathy with them, as they repeated to one another the words of the prophet: "Surely he hath borne our griefs, and carried our sorrows."

But this darkness was a testimony in favor of Christ, and in condemnation of his enemies. At his baptism, the heavens were opened to him. On the mount of transfiguration, he had a celestial appearance. But God is now testifying to him by a different miracle. He who formed the light on Tabor, now created darkness, to make the unbelieving world confess, as the centurion did, Truly this was the Son of God. The enemies of Christianity have endeavored to do away the impression which this miracle was suited to make, but in vain do they oppose conjectures and the silence of some contemporary writers, to the express declarations of the Evangelists, who wrote so near the time of the alleged event, that a false assertion with regard to a phenomenon like this would have been instantly turned to their discomfiture. Such a man as Josephus, a prejudiced Jew, could not consistently mention a thing which testifies so powerfully in behalf of Christ. It is indeed charitable in some, to account for this silence by supposing that the darkness, though noticeable, was no more than has ordinarily happened in what have been called dark days. But we can hardly suppose that the Evangelists, as mere writers of history, would speak of a natural darkness in connection with things which, if they happened at all, must have been miraculous. Moreover, though the Christian fathers were divided as to the extent of this darkness, there is evidence that it was not confined to Judæa. The well-known exclamation of Dionysius, the Areopagite, in Egypt, recorded by a historian, is not the only proof of this, when he said, "Either the Deity is suffering, or one is suffering with whom the Deity sympathizes."

To admit this darkness to be miraculous, is to confess that God acknowledged Jesus as the Messiah. It gives great confirmation to faith, to know that heaven thus acknowledged the Redeemer while in the act of expiating our guilt.

To the enemies of Christ, this must have been an appalling spectacle. They did not know enough about astronomy to consider that the position of the heavenly bodies did not cause it, but they must have been impressed with the coincidence that darkness, even if caused naturally, should have come on just at that time; and as wicked people are superstitious, they must have been deeply moved; "the heathen are dismayed at the signs of heaven," and these murderers, also, must have been impressed with the thought that heaven was bearing witness against them. Perhaps some, if not many, of them relented, and then the centurion at the cross expressed the convictions and the repentance of a multitude, the beginning of whose faith at the crucifixion was confirmed by the resurrection, and in whom, with others, this prophecy will there be seen to have been, in part, fulfilled, "When thou shalt make his soul an offering for sin, he shall see his seed."

This darkness shows that nature and the moral universe are in sympathy. When the law was given, there were thunderings and lightnings; when Israel was to be delivered from Egypt, fire, hail, and darkness afflicted the land; and at the passage of the Red Sea, as we learn from the seventy-seventh Psalm, there were great signs in nature: "the voice of thy thunder was in the

4

heavens; the lightnings lightened the world; the earth trembled and shook." At the resurrection of Christ, "behold, there was a great earthquake;" at the day of judgment, the heavens are to be on fire, the elements will melt with fervent heat, the earth and all that is therein will be burned up. The God of nature is the God of salvation; the God of grace is the great and terrible God, and if nature gave such signs when he redeemed us, how will it be at the last and dreadful day?

It is pleasant to think, as we sit at the Lord's table, of the contrast in the scene with that of the crucifixion. Nature is not convulsed; we are not disturbed by insulting voices; the darkness is past, a clear light shines. Nor are we unsuitably affected by the agonizing sight of the Sufferer, in which respect we are compelled to feel that the Romish Church is painfully wrong. Her object in her little chapels at the road side, with figures of the crucifixion in them, throughout the Roman Catholic world, and by her representations in her churches, is continually to show the suffering Christ to the eye; and this is carried to excess. With her, Jesus seems to be still on the cross. It is not with sectarian prejudice that we express the belief that there is a melancholic and depressing effect upon pious feeling by her disproportionate view of the Saviour's agony, such as the experience of the Apostles surely does not sustain; for if they had given us pictures and images of

Christ corresponding to the tone of their Epistles, and as the Saviour himself chose to present himself before the eye of John in Patmos, heavenly exaltation and majesty, triumph and joy, would have shared largely with the crucifixion in their impressions upon our senses. We are glad to be delivered from the controlling, the limiting, effect of pictures in worship, and to trust ourselves and to have the pious mind even in the lowest stages of intelligence, trust itself, to the full scope of the imagination as an aid to faith, rather than receive dictation from imagery in worship. Things comprehensible are aided in their effect upon us by their representative images, but things of an infinite nature cannot be expressed by signs, however good, without making the thoughts grovel. It is a part of our Protestant privilege, in which we greatly rejoice for its effect upon mental activity in spiritual things, that we are not under bondage, in our worship, to any visible delineations.

The true greatness of the event which we commemorate at the Lord's table, is impressively taught by these marvels. God never does any thing out of proportion. It was therefore not a teacher, nor a martyr who was dying, when the heavens were spread with sackcloth; he was more than man who expired on the tree; his sufferings and death were more than the sufferings of one who came to set men an example. The scenery was exaggerated if only a good man and a prophet were dying.

If darkness came to mingle her dreary influence even amid the scenes of love and mercy on the cross, surely nothing can prevent the perfect usurpation of her power over those who finally reject that mercy, and are not won by that love. Even now, to those who do not receive Christ and his sacrifice for their sins, the doctrines of the Gospel, not being viewed in connection with that sacrifice, are dark; the understanding is darkened, the future is dark, and so is the providence of God. That scriptural emblem of the forlorn state of the wicked, darkness, conveys a fearful idea of their future condition. Long and tedious are the night-watches on a sick-bed, when we toss to and fro, with no power to sleep, and a disordered fancy fills us with direful images, and the morning seems as though it would never come. But what must it be to lie down in sorrow and endless night, where the daystar never rises, and the night grows darker and darker, and despair peoples it with horrors.

But to the believer, the darkness of the crucifixion is only an emblem of that darkest time of night which, according to the proverb, is just before day. By thy death, O Saviour, in the midst of darkness and sorrows, we shall soon pass from under these shades and their gloom, to those scenes where they need no candle, neither light of the sun, for the Lord God giveth them light, and they shall reign for ever and ever.

The darkness of the crucifixion had a limit. The

sure moment was marked by the hand of God when the shades should be dispelled, and light and joy return to the earth. In times of darkness and sorrow, we will look to him who went from the shades of death to perfect and endless joy. One of his ministers was preaching from these words: "Behold, Satan shall cast some of you into prison, and ye shall have tribulation ten days. Be thou faithful unto death, and I will give thee a crown of life." A humble woman in great trouble, was deeply impressed by the limit which the text seemed so absolutely to fix in that particular instance of Satan's power; and as she passed along the street, she was heard to say, "Blessed be His name it cannot be eleven." Our sufferings will be for so many days, and no more; "surely there shall be an end, and thy expectation shall not be cut off." However dark our condition and prospects may seem, no darkness can visit our souls like that which came upon the soul of Christ, and wrung from him amidst the darkness of the heavens that outcry on the tree. But in that moment the agonizing work of suffering for sin was finished, and light began to break over a ransomed world.

II. THE RENDING OF THE VAIL.

"AND BEHOLD THE VAIL OF THE TEMPLE WAS RENT IN TWAIN FROM THE TOP TO THE BOTTOM."

In the pale light, the divine sufferer was seen upon his cross between the thieves. "Jesus, when he had cried again with a loud voice, yielded up the ghost. And behold the vail of the temple was rent in twain from the top to the bottom."

Simple and brief as these few words are, they relate one of the most significant and important events in the history of the world.

This vail, as originally made, and, no doubt, imitated in the second temple, was the innermost of two curtains of "blue and purple and scarlet and fine twined linen," in front of the Holy of holies.

None but the high-priest could enter or look within this vail, and he only once a year. At that stated season, the small bells on the high-priest's vesture were heard along the aisle of the temple toward the Holy place; and then within the outer sanctuary, till they ceased behind that sacred vail. Not even heaven itself, perhaps, was more sacred in the eye of a Jew than that sequestered, mysterious spot, concealed by the vail. It would be death to any mortal who should presume to look with curious eye into its dread retirement. The most exalted religious personage of the nation stood alone with the God of all the earth, and offered the appointed blood of atonement. No les, inviolable therefore, than the presence of God, did that vail seem to the whole Jewish people. To see the vail of the firmament torn asunder, disclosing the third heavens, would not have been more surprising to them than the Holy of holies opened to the public gaze.

The fulness of time had come. The incarnate Word was upon the cross, accomplishing, by his one sacrifice for sin, the object of the types and ordinances under the law. He cried again with a loud voice, and yielded up the ghost. At that moment, this sacred, impenetrable vail was, without hands, rent asunder from top to bottom. They who were watching, or doing service, in the temple, were no doubt attracted by the noise to the spot, and there the inviolable covering of the Holy of holies was hanging in two pieces, and the sight which only one mortal eye from time to time was permitted to behold, lay open to the common gaze. We may imagine the feelings of Caiaphas as he looked upon that rent vail. Well might he have rent his own garments. There was no more any Holy of holies. The earthquake did not so much astound the people as this rending of the vail. They had felt earthquakes before, but since the destruction of the first temple, and the Holy of holies with it, by fire, no such event as this, so mysteriously significant with regard to their religion, had transpired. What was that death, that outcry on the tree, that yielding up the ghost, which rent that vail? Was this the death of a martyr? Is a good man finishing his testimony and his life together? No, the Lamb of God is taking away the sin of the world; he is dismissing the sacrifices, he is displacing Aaron and his sons, he has become himself the offering and the priest. O Lord, what are we that we should be permitted to commemorate that event by showing forth that death, as though it had application to us. Yes, for us that vail was rent. The dim outlines of the great sacrifice, which were seen in the temple service, change to a substantial form; the shadow of him who was to come no longer holds us in painful expectation, but the author and finisher of our faith is here. No priests are needed now for man with God. He who pretends to be a priest, now, and to offer sacrifice for sins, does an empty service, he holds an antiquated office. He is a torchbearer, a lamplighter, in the daytime; he must contrive darkness, in order to make employment for himself. The vail of the temple gave up the ghost of all the sacrifices and offerings when the Saviour died. Perhaps the unbelieving priests employed themselves to mend that rent vail; their occupation would be gone for ever did they not keep up a mystery in connection with the Holy of holies. But when Christ died, their whole service, once so sacred, became a dead body; yet to this day there are those who practise their curious arts to make it seem alive. We come, O joyful thought, at every communion season, to behold those ceremonies fulfilled by him who is made priest not by a carnal commandment, but after the power of an endless life. He has indeed entered within the vail, but it is a vail which instead of inclosing a dread solitude, includes the world of glorified spirits, and the innumerable company of angels, a place from which we are not debarred; for we have boldness to enter into the holiest by the blood of Jesus, and may draw near with a true heart in full assurance of faith.

III. THE EARTHQUAKE.

"AND THE EARTH DID QUAKE, AND THE ROCKS RENT."

Had this earthquake occurred in all respects by the ordinary operations of nature, such a coincidence, in that dread hour, with the miraculous signs, would have been hardly less impressive than a miracle; and there would be room to question whether it required less credulity to believe the coincidence than the supernatural sign. But believing all which we do respecting the divine Saviour, those convulsions of nature bring a solemn awe over our minds as we reflect that the great transaction, which moved the foundations of the earth, was on our account; and that each of us had as great a personal interest in it as any human being. There is an interesting narrative, by an early writer on Palestine, of a deist, who was converted to Christianity by contemplating a principal rock near Calvary, which had evidently been rent in a direction contrary to geological laws. It is a common remark, that our hearts, if they do not feel the power of Christ's death, are harder than the rocks; but when we think who Christ is, and what his death implies, it would seem that the inhabitants of other worlds would find it more difficult to believe that every heart is not broken with sorrow for sin, by the Saviour's death, than it ever was for a deist to believe that the rocks rent when he died.

IV. THE OPENING OF THE GRAVES.

"AND THE GRAVES WERE OPENED; AND MANY BODIES OF SAINTS WHICH SLEPT AROSE, AND CAME OUT OF THE GRAVES AFTER HIS RESURRECTION, AND WENT INTO THE HOLY CITY, AND APPEARED UNTO MANY."

While the sepulchres hewn in rocks were some of them shattered and opened by the expiring cry of Jesus, it is supposed by judicious writers that the occupants of them did not rise till Christ had risen, though the construction of the words, as in some other instances, by disregarding the order of time, would make a different impression. Others, however, think that the dead arose at the voice of Christ, but did not present themselves to public notice till the Saviour had risen.

These saints must, some of them at least, have been such as would be recognized by relatives and friends, or else the power of the miracle would have been lost. But their reappearance, surely, was not to gratify curiosity nor desire.

Was it a pleasure to see these departed friends restored to life? What a mixture of emotions it must have created. What sluices of sorrow, what wounds, would be opened by the reappearance of the dead. What information could they give of death and heaven? We may venture to say, None. Had any knowledge of the unseen world been thus imparted, it would have been caught with the utmost avidity, and been transmitted from age to age. It is probable, therefore, that on the return of these souls to their bodies, they could relate nothing in detail respecting the separate state. When Paul had been caught up to the third heavens, as he could not tell at the time whether he was in the body or out of the body, so he says that the things which he heard were "unspeakable things," as well as "not lawful for man to utter." After all, it was but a short-lived pleasure, if any, derived from the reappearance of those departed friends; the thought of another separation would drink up all the joy of a temporary sojourn, as now the anguish of separation for some time counterbalances all the pleasure of a happy life. Should we be willing, if we could, to meet departed friends at the Lord's table? If we reflect upon it, we shall probably conclude that it is far better for us, with our sufficient knowledge imparted by a written and completed revelation, not to have the silence broken, nor the separation interrupted.

What, then, was the wisdom, the benevolence, of this resurrection at the time of Christ's death? It kindly assisted the infant faith of Christian believers. It was a republication of Job's assurance, "Though after my skin worms destroy this body, yet in my flesh shall I see God." It furnished a demonstration of the rising from the dead, as not only possible, but as being connected with Christ. The Apostles and the early believers must have had strong consolation by means of those risen saints with regard to their own resurrection. Christ rose, and brought with him a lifeguard from the dead. Not only were Christians thus reassured that Christ was the Messiah, but also that those who sleep in Jesus, God will bring with him. It is difficult to suppose that these risen saints died again; the common belief is that they ascended to heaven; and if so, while Christ was still the first-fruits of them that slept, here were his sheaves with him, in advance, from the harvest at the end of the world. As such, they must have contributed to the joy and exultation of saints in heaven, who are still waiting for the adoption, to wit, the redemption of their bodies.

This miracle is to us most interesting and instructive, because each of us is hereafter to experience, at the voice of Christ, that which is here told of these dead bodies and departed souls. He who by his last utterance on the cross, opened those graves, will, by the next voice of his, which we shall hear, open our graves. Something else will then be "finished," and that is, His mediatorial office, the power of his death to atone for sin. To-day, the Christian at the table, to-day those who go away from the sight of the table, may each reflect, that He who died for him on Calvary, and opened the graves by his expiring cry, will bid each of them leave his separate state, and wait by the side of the grave for his rising body. Perhaps the last descendant of yours who could feel any obligation or interest leading him to protect and cherish your grave, will have died, and that burying-place may be smoothed into undistinguished likeness with the general earth; the marble, and the iron fences, may have perished; but your body will be there. All that are in their graves shall hear his voice and shall come forth. From the table spread with the memorials of the body and blood which on Calvary atoned for our sins, that same voice calls to each of us, and says, "This do in remembrance of me." We would be found of him in peace at his coming;

we must therefore have a state of feeling which will lead us to show forth his death. And so being planted together with him in the likeness of his death, we shall be also in the likeness of his resurrection.

IV.

THE THREE CROSSES.

"I AM CRUCIFIED WITH CHRIST."
"BY WHOM THE WORLD IS CRUCIFIED UNTO ME AND I UNTO THE WORLD."

HERE are three crosses, the same as on Mount Calvary. But who are these which are represented as crucified with Christ? One is a Christian. The other is the world. The Christian says, I am crucified with Christ; and speaking of Christ, he says, By whom the world is crucified unto me and I unto the world.

He who uttered those words, declares himself to be beyond the power of the world to awaken his desires and efforts for any happiness superior to that which is derived from knowing and serving Christ. To be crucified is not, primarily, to be put to death; it is to be affixed to a cross. The world had thus been treated in a certain sense by Paul. He had placed it on a cross; meaning, that instead of its having full power to engage his affections, it was like a crucified person who is devoted to a shameful death. Such a person had any other effect than that of fascination upon the beholder. It was so with the world as to its power over Paul's mind.

He adds, —'and I unto the world.' The world has lost its power to fascinate me, as though I were hanging on a cross. If enticing pleasures should present themselves to one hanging on a cross, they could not awaken desire in his mind. He was in such a state that the world had no power to govern his affections, and had withdrawn from him in some respects, as from one who is separated from the world by the cross.

Paul could pass through the streets of such a place as Corinth, and even dwell there, and not be drawn aside by its intoxicating pleasures, nor be made ashamed of his religion with its crucified Lord, by the pride of learning and all the accomplishments for which the city was famous. That place whose preëminent wealth and luxury a Roman poet alludes to, when he says, "It does not happen to every man to go to Corinth," affected the Apostle only with compassion for its sins. He was not, however, a misanthrope; he took no gloomy views of the world; he looked at things in their true light. Such was his superiority to the various forms of pleasure which Athens afforded, that of its thousands of altars, with their splendid rites, in many cases, of eloquence and music, and wealth and beauty, he was attracted by none save that which superstition had reared to the unknown God. He was more concerned for the ignorance and sins of the people indicated by that altar, than charmed by that beautiful place. This is but one illustration of the state of his mind. The world was a crucified thing to him, and he was dead to the world. Yet he had not succeeded, like a hermit, in steeling himself against the power of the world. He was as sensible as ever to every excellence, and had not lost his eyes, nor ears, nor his taste, by being a Christian. After reading his two Epistles to the Corinthians, which are not surpassed by any thing from his pen, it is interesting to think of that disclaimer with which his address begins, that he did not come to Corinth with "excellency of speech." Yet if the rhetoricians of that city had, any of them, left among their writings such a piece as that of Paul on the Resurrection, not to mention other parts of these epistles, it would have held rank for 'excellency of speech' with any thing which the Greek moralists have bequeathed to us. Paul was therefore by no means insensible to excellence of any kind as he found it in the world, but his superior love to Christ created that state of his affections of which he speaks when he says, "By whom the world is crucified unto me, and I unto the world."

Paul had a clear, affecting sense of Christ's love to him. Though his religious experience, in the beginning of it, was peculiar in consequence of the Saviour's personal appearance to him on the road to Damascus, this was not the principal thing which convinced him of that love. This was the "faithful saying, worthy of all acceptation, that Christ Jesus came into the world to save sinners." The death of Christ as an expiation for sin, had more influence over Paul's mind, than all other truths; the idea of what he calls justification by faith, the possibility of forgiving sin consistently with great interests at stake, and of doing it in a way which not only manifests infinite love, but awakens and perpetuates love of the most powerful kind, and, in the most effectual manner, secures the highest obedience of the forgiven, was, as a philosophy, as a governmental arrangement, as well as an act of mercy and love, and an expedient resulting in the highest honor of God and the largest amount of human happiness, sufficient to fill the mind and heart of this man with supreme pleasure. And when this truth gets full possession of any mind, that the divine Word became a sacrifice for sins, that he loved us and gave himself for us, there is nothing of which we ever heard, the imagination never pictured any thing, which deserves to be compared with it. This was with Paul a living, abiding reality; he had no double-mindedness in his faith; the sceptics of his day did not shake his belief, nor did he need to read every thing which might be written, to be sure that some neologist had not discovered an objection to his system which could not be refuted. "I know whom I have believed, and am persuaded that he is able to keep that which I have committed unto him against that day." The assurance that Christ loved him and died for him, (though in no sense in which he has not suffered and died for us,) held him steadfast in his faith; and this absorbed his affections. So it is in every case in which we are persuaded of our obligations to Christ, and of the infinite, personal benefit derived from him. This is the way in which the world becomes crucified to us and we to the world. It is not by striving to hate the world, nor by efforts to withdraw ourselves from it. When a strong affection takes possession of us, all other objects inconsistent with it are really crucified to us, and we are crucified to them. We see this in friendship and love, and in attachments to engrossing pursuits.

It is moreover evident from Paul's writings, that the matchless excellence of the Saviour's character extinguished his supreme love for all other objects. His feelings never kindle as when he speaks of Christ. He had such pleasure in the knowledge already gained of Christ, that he counted all things but loss for the excellency of that knowledge. The mystery of God and man in the Saviour's person, is, indeed, the most awakening of all revealed truths. Moreover, perfection is, in Christ, reduced to the scale of human feelings and conduct, while, added to the human qualities of the Saviour, deity appears, exciting further desires to know him. It is, therefore, natural that the character of Christ should awaken stronger feelings than any other object in a mind which fully perceives and loves it. The experience of good men everywhere confirms this. When they express their feelings toward Christ in their hymns, they show a kind and degree of love never exceeded. There is a charm in the character of Christ for a mind that appreciates him, which can expel the supreme love of every thing else.

Paul was conscious of receiving benefits from Christ, which, as an intellectual and moral being, he felt, laid him under the greatest obligations. It was by Christ that he was led to see his true character as an accountable being, and the relation in which he stood to God. Up to that time, his self-knowledge was mainly an error. Now he had views of himself which he never had before, was made acquainted with his own mind and heart in a way which, to such a man, must have been more interesting than any other knowledge. As we read his account of his religious experience in the seventh of Romans, we perceive that his awakening to a true knowledge of himself was esteemed by him a benefit which no earthly honor or pleasure could equal. His convictions of sin were an invaluable means of self-knowledge, and they made him acquainted with the great system of truth which from that time began to unfold itself to his view. When he saw that God would not suffer him to make satisfaction to divine justice, but required him to believe on him who justifies the ungodly; when he perceived that it was possible for God not to impute his trespasses to him, and that He would save him as a helpless sinner through grace, he is astonished at the wisdom, the love, the condescension of this plan, harmonizing justice with mercy; he is lost in wonder at the method of sacrifice and suffering by which it was effected. He knew, then, for the first time, the exquisite pleasure of repentance. He experienced that which discipline and self-control never did for him, for by the power of regeneration, his passions, for the first time, were like the seas when the moon assumed her rule over them by the tides. For the first time in his life he loved God; now for the first time it could be said of him, Behold, he prayeth. The consciousness of increasing likeness to God, of communion with him, and of the joys of a Christian life, of being useful, of exerting an influence for the honor of God, as well as for the highest happiness of men in the world to come as well as this, had the natural effect to give him that indifference to all things else, which he describes by saying that he and worldly things are crucified the one to the other.

His expectations and hopes, also, were a powerful means of producing and perpetuating this state of mind. Heaven was the object of his supreme desire, for there he would be with Christ. In thinking of death and the grave he found that they had lost their terrors.

Nothing seems to fill his thoughts or excite his imagination more, than the resurrection of the dead.

We may add to the influences which wrought the effect we are contemplating, upon the mind of Paul, the power that must have proceeded from the work in which he was engaged. Honest industry of every kind is fatal to luxury. It is well said that "work is the salt of the mind." Occupied as he was with an employment which stimulated every power and faculty both of mind and body, inferior things found no relish in him, and he had no time for their fascinations. No man could more truly say, One thing I do. The absorbing power of his employment was, however, due to its being derived from such sources as we have already considered.

Let it be supposed that the reader is one to whom the world seems cheerful and bright, whose hopes and prospects fill the heart with the most pleasurable emotions, or the actual gratification of whose affections in themselves innocent, is the source of thrilling pleasure. It is proposed to such an one to be a Christian. It is most probable that the thought would be repulsive, and be regarded as inconsistent with present and allowable happiness. Perhaps the idea of being "crucified" to the world, and having the world crucified to us, occurs to the mind as the proper and inevitable effect of being a Christian. Is religion suited to one on the eve of perfect earthly joy or in the rapturous possession of the heart's desire? We know that it is good in affliction, exceedingly proper at mature and sober years, and indispensable in death. But was it ever designed for one who has all that heart can wish within reach, or in possession? How would we persuade a beloved friend in these circumstances that this is so?

Your calculations for happiness are all made, your image of earthly bliss is formed, you are expecting to be perfectly happy. If one should say to you that 'all which cometh is vanity,' that is, fleeting, perishable, that our desires for happiness are never satisfied by the world, that we still crave something better than the most perfect earthly bliss, and even this may at any moment be dashed from our embrace, it would all be true, but your answer would probably be, that you are willing to take this risk, receive things as they come, and stand in your lot. There is, therefore, a more sat-factory way of presenting the subject. You are permitted by the God who formed you with these susceptibilities, to be happy in the innocent gratification of all your desires; he does not grudge you this happiness; he does not lie in wait to rob you of it, but, in the enjoyment or the anticipation of your heart's desire, he informs you that there is a happiness which alone can give a satisfying pleasure to other joys. Most unaccountable would it be if the God who made us capable of pleasure, had no power to make us happier in knowing and loving him, than by any of his gifts. There are no circumstances of human joy to which the consciousness of loving God is not a pleasurable addition. Not only so, there is no pleasure which beforehand, or in the enjoyment of it, or in retrospection, is not deficient without the love of God.

Then it is furthermore true that as the love of God is the only satisfying happiness, it creates distaste for other things which are inconsistent with it. God is an enemy to nothing which is not an enemy to him; we in like manner, by loving him, become indisposed to nothing which would be for our good. To become a Christian, therefore, is not the violent and unnatural disruption of attachments, and the sacrifice of happiness, and the exchange of gladness for austerity which some suppose. They think that in being religious, they must first be stripped of every thing which they love, and pass over to some untried objects which they cannot force themselves to love. Let them at once love the Redeemer of the world, as Paul did, and for the same reasons, which in no respect were more pertinent in his case than in theirs, and they will not be conscious of expelling their sinful attachments, but as the growth of the perfect flower breaks open and throws aside the old embracement which seemed essential to it, so the heart which receives Christ and religion, parts, without reluctance, with former sinful pleasures and attachments. This is true in the first experience of religious feelings; but afterwards temptation arises, the flesh lusts against the spirit, and through life there is a conflict. But the conscience and the judgment take part with spiritual things, the renewed heart continues to find its only satisfying pleasure in them, the motives derived, especially, from the consideration of Christ, lead us to view ourselves and the world as Paul did when he speaks of being crucified to the world and of the world as crucified to him. Not that he is dead to the world, but dying; not that the world is dead or ceases to importune, but the world is on its cross consigned to death; and as Christ died for sin on our account, every motive of gratitude and love, every desire to be like him, constrains us also to be, as it were, on the cross. Nor is it perpetual agony, as the figure would seem to represent. Beautifully does the Apostle explain this: "I am crucified with Christ; nevertheless I live; yet not I, but Christ liveth in me; and the life which I now live in the flesh I live by the faith of the Son of God, who loved me, and gave himself for me." When he says, 'nevertheless, I live,' he means, I know, in its highest sense, now, what it is to live; indeed, it is as though Christ lived, thought, acted in me, and by me, not constraining me against my will, but through my grateful submission of my all to him, who loved me and gave himself for me. Let those who dread the sacrifice and suffering which they imagine are required by religion, through self-denial, consider, that love for an endeared object is not conscious of self-denial or suffering, that in our devoted attachments we sustain the heaviest burdens, and perform labors and offices of kindness which wealth could not procure; and so it is in religion which is actuated, as true religion always is, by love to Christ. Let him who dreads it, have experience of it in its power to resist and subdue sin. He will say as a revered and lamented missionary said, in his last moments, "I did not know that it was so easy to die." *

But supposing that religion were only the experience of stern suffering in obedience to Christ, that through life no joy visited our hearts; or, that while we had great spiritual satisfaction and pleasure, as Christ must have had, in doing our duty, it were necessary to separate ourselves from the world and from every thing in it which gratified our feelings. If Christ died for us as the only method of atoning for our transgressions, surely we should not refuse to suffer with him; if for us he was a man of sorrows and acquainted with grief, how could we, if required, decline to endure any thing which might be made to appear right and proper? In that sense we should be willing to be crucified to the world and to have the world crucified to us.

So that when we read that "with him they crucify two thieves, the one on his right hand, the other on his left," we may each of us see himself and the world represented truly by those malefactors, we saying, as

* Rev. John Scudder, M. D., Madras.

one of them did, 'And we indeed justly, for we receive the due reward of our deeds.' Each of us, could he have paid the forfeiture of his sins by being crucified, and suffering as Jesus did, would have been permitted to do it if divine mercy had been willing to save us in this way. But we could not atone for our sins, even by crucifixion; the death of Christ was not a substitute for our crucifixion, but for our endless misery. "All mankind by the fall, lost communion with God, are under his wrath and curse, and so made liable to all the miseries of this life, to death itself, and to the pains of hell forever." Instead of its being productive of the richest and sweetest pleasures known to the human heart to be, in the sense explained, crucified with Christ, our life on earth would justly have been a protracted anguish, perpetual darkness would have covered us while we made expiation for our sins, and an agony like that of him who bore our load, would have wrung from us continually the cry, Father, if this cup may not pass from us except we drink it, thy will be done.

But now when we say, I am crucified with Christ, and profess that the world is crucified to us, we recognize that which is the only true source of all wisdom and happiness, of likeness to Christ, and perfect redemption. If, therefore, at any time, our corruptions struggle for the mastery, and the world tempts us to forget or forsake Christ, we may well remember that our proper place at such moments of temptation would be, with the tempting world, at the side of the dying Redeemer, crucified with him. There let that tempting world be fixed by us, and then let it assail, or court, or upbraid us; we, each of us a penitent thief upon a cross by the Saviour's side, within sight and hearing of all that he suffers for us, can certainly endure temptation; surely we can watch with him one hour; the sins which he is atoning for, we will not commit, or repeat, to his face; the sacrifice and service he requires as a testimony of our love, we shall not fail to render. Those three crosses on Mount Calvary may therefore stand before the eye of every follower of Christ, as memorials and emblems of his progress in redemption in this life, of his profession, of the infinite cost of sin, and the highest motive to die unto it, and to live unto righteousness.

V.

MEMBERSHIP IN CHRIST.

"FOR WE ARE MEMBERS OF HIS BODY, OF HIS FLESH, AND OF HIS BONES."

SUCH language would greatly mislead, were there not something most intimate and peculiar in the relation between Christ and his people. The idea is, that there is the most perfect union and identification of all believers with Christ, such as can be expressed only by speaking of us, not merely as members of his body, but of his flesh and of his bones. Why this latter intensified particularity? It is warranted, we shall find, by the representations of the Bible.

We must take those enlarged views of redemption which the epistles of the New Testament present, if we would arrive at a higher degree of faith, and greater comfort; for if we dwell inordinately upon our individual unimportance, or our individual demerit, we fail to view ourselves in connection with a stupendous system which gives us dignity and bliss as a necessary result of its plan. When the glory of God, and not man, becomes, in our view, the end of redemption, we see that man is of necessity raised by it to privileges and honors which he cannot account for, which he cannot believe, if he confines his thoughts merely to his rank in creation, or to his ill desert. God is evidently using this our race to illustrate great principles, and to effect great purposes connected with the eternal interests of the universe. What is sin, what are its effects on the whole nature of the sinner; the consistency of mercy and pardon with justice, not in exceptional cases, but under a system of forgiveness through an atonement; the wonderful harmony between divine efficiency, and the perfect free agency of the creature; the love and compassion of God; the wonders of the cross; the effect upon the whole moral being of restoration from a fallen, depraved state, to a higher condition of bliss than was lost; and withal the direful influence of sin in the desperate resistance by some of all the means and motives employed to save them; then the just, the terrible consequences of unforgiven sin, illustrated forever in the punishment of those who refused to be saved; — to illustrate these things will be among the results, and is now the object, of redemption. While the lost will greatly illustrate certain important principles in the government of God, it is in those that are saved that his character will be principally exhibited. So the Scriptures everywhere teach. Hence, redeemed men are necessary to His great plan; God loves them, prizes them, honors them, in some respect, as a man does his materials, implements, and the products of his labor. As men feel toward the precious stones, or the gold and silver, or the costly wood which are to compose their fabrics, or the fruits and rare flowers on which they have expended great toil, or the productions of their genius, so, from infinitely higher considerations, the redeemed are identified with the glory of God in his thoughts of them. "Since thou wast precious in my sight, thou hast been honorable, and I have loved thee." "I have redeemed thee; thou art mine." Not only is it true that God is our portion, but we are his, —"the Lord's portion is his people." Now, if we merely look at ourselves as poor, weak, sinful worms of the dust, we may well despair; it requires no small measure of faith to believe that we ever can become truly great and good; yet in the same way might the unsightly mineral think and reason, though destined to become a principal diamond on the brow of a queen.

Surely if we think what endless variety of beauty and glory inert matter, in its most unpromising shapes, assumes, under the forming and adorning hand of God, we may cease to doubt that our spirits, once his image, are capable of something more than our perverted, blind hearts dare to hope for. Of matter, all the diversified objects of sight, and sound, and touch, and smell, and taste, are made, wrought by infinite skill into a limitless variety of forms. The God who uses matter thus, can make man, body and soul, to exceed all his perfect conceptions of himself, and compel his wearied fancy to confess, "It doth not yet appear what we shall be."

There is a beautiful figure connected with this topic in the Epistle of James. "Of his own will begat he us by the word of truth that we should be a kind of first-fruits of his creatures." The first ripe fruit, the cluster of grapes, and even the unexpected appearance of an early vegetable, or a new sheaf, fills one with pleasure. We are to be a 'kind of first-fruits' among the creatures of God, exciting delight as proofs of infinite efforts, infinite wisdom, and astonishing success. We must therefore think of ourselves in connection with Redemption as being each a subject and an illustration of the mediatorial government of God, something on which He is to exercise infinite love and power. Poor, degraded, lost soul, — in your own esteem, — you are to Him what a pearl is to the eye of the pearl-diver among the weeds and mire of the sea. Wherever the grace of God has changed a soul into his own image, there is invested a degree of worth with which the mines of all the earth hold no parallel. But all this is merely preliminary to more important considerations. It simply shows us that when the Bible speaks of the perfect identification of Christ and his people, (members of his body, of his flesh, and of his bones,) it is warranted by the relation which Christians sustain to the mediatorial kingdom of God.

We come, however, to a more specific view of what the Bible says concerning our membership in Christ, as we remember that Christ sees in us who believe, the special objects for which he suffered and died. " He is the Saviour of all men, specially of those that believe."

We should intensely love those for whom we should die. How the martyrs loved Christ! We know how Ignatius, going into the Roman theatre to be devoured of lions, for Christ's sake, poured out his soul to Jesus. John Huss of Bohemia, burning at the stake, sung a hymn which was heard above the roaring flames, and as he was expiring he cried, Come, Lord Jesus. Lambert, the martyr, when they offered him the crucifix, to worship it before they lighted the flames, joyfully exclaimed, None but Christ, none but Christ. Thus, and infinitely more, did Christ love you, and died for you. He looks upon his people, each and all, as the fruit of his coming into the world, the objects of his sufferings, his agonies. He associates them with his victory over death and the grave, his ascension, and with his glory, for, as one who loves another loves to have that friend know and share his bliss, Christ said, " Father, I will that those whom thou hast given me be with me where I am, that they may behold my glory which thou hast given me." Whatever He is as a Saviour they are essential to it. He could not be a Saviour without them; they are identified with him as the flesh and bones are identified with the person of a human being.

It makes this seem natural and easy when we consider among other things that Christ and we have the same nature. In all points as we are, without sin, He is as really one with us as the head with the members of the body. Whatever joys his human nature is now capable of, he knows that we, in the same circumstances, would be capable of the same. "Who shall change our vile body that it may be fashioned like unto his glorious body." "When he shall appear, we shall be like him, for we shall see him as he is."

The language of Scripture corresponds with this — "joint heirs with Christ;" "ye are Christ's, and Christ is God's," in which a comparison, a simile, is evidently implied. "I will declare thy name unto my brethren." "Behold, I, and the children which thou hast given me." These are the words of Christ.

The intimate communion which Christ is represented as maintaining with his people agrees with this: "He that loveth me shall be loved of my Father, and I will love him, and will manifest myself to him." "I will come in to him and sup with him and he with me."

Perhaps the greatest confirmation of the subject is found in the Lord's Supper. Perfect identification, which cannot be exceeded, is expressed by eating the flesh and drinking the blood of Christ. By this, so far as a symbol can do it, we, on our part, identify him with our flesh, our bones; and surely, if this be permitted, it is because He has first identified us with himself, — "because He first loved us."

So perfect did Christ regard the oneness between himself and us that he speaks of it on this wise: "As the living Father hath sent me, and I live by the Father, so he that eateth me shall live by me." "Whoso eateth my flesh and drinketh my blood hath eternal life, and I will raise him up at the last day."

If I am a Christian, I am one of those by whom God has purposed to show his character in the work of redemption. True, I am only one, and that, perhaps, an inferior one. So the particle of gold might say as it is rolled along over the pebbles toward the gold-hunter, — I am only one piece, and a small piece of gold, — but the eye of that man will recognize it, his hand will eagerly seize it, he sailed over the seas for just this kind of thing.

If I am a Christian, God has made me so. Blessed truth! something more than my own change of my governing purpose took place when I became a Christian; my repentance, faith, the whole of my own agency was indispensable, but, there is a work of the Spirit; — "nor of the will of man, but of God." God has created me in Christ Jesus. If so, He thought it worth the effort, He had a purpose in it; I am given to Christ; Christ has recognized me — now his honor, his word, his cause, stand pledged for my safety in connection with my persevering efforts. Striving against sin, and overcoming, my redemption will be a part of his triumph; his final glory and joy will be mine. Now I see the truth of those great promises—"All things are yours, whether the world, or life, or death, or things present or things to come, all are yours; and ye are Christ's and Christ is God's." "Who shall separate us from the love of Christ?" "Him that overcometh will I grant to sit with me in my throne."

Some one, perhaps he is a Christian, will say, "If this be so, there must be great forbearance and compassion in the love of Christ to his people, for there are those at the table with me to-day who are exceedingly imperfect, to me unlovely, but perhaps in the judgment of charity they are Christians. How are they one with Christ?" He died for them, nevertheless, and is redeeming them. He loves them, and will present them "faultless before the presence of his glory with exceeding joy." These are such as he came to save, and to do this he identifies them with himself. Perhaps an additional reflection will make the forbearance and compassion of Christ still more wonderful. 'I take it for granted,' you may say, 'that Christ loves me.' Certainly, how mnch superior you are to these. But is this certain? That very feeling, that repugnance to weaker Christians, that avoidance of them, that intolerance of their peculiarities, may make it more difficult for Christ to love you than them. This is not the spirit of Christ, but is contrary to it, for he condescends to men of low estate, and it may be my estate was so low, my sins, my unworthiness were such that, as angels saw him coming to me, they might have said, What condescension, what forbearance, what compassion, to set his love on that sinner. Perhaps when you reach heaven you will see, that to overcome such a proud heart as yours, to bear and forbear with you, has nothing beyond it among the miracles of grace, and there will be no redeemed sinner there but you would then be willing to wash his feet, in testimony that Christ condescended as much in saving you as him.

'You lay great obligations upon us,' I hear you say, 'if these things be so.' But in what way?—'Surely,' you reply, 'if there be this identification between Christ and me, what manner of person ought I to be in all holy conversation and godliness. I must walk worthily of such union. If all this be true, surely I live, yet not I but Christ liveth in me. I must not sin.' "Know ye not that ye are the temple of God, and that the spirit of God dwelleth in you?" "Shall I take the members of Christ and make them the members of an harlot?" "If any man defile the temple of God, him shall God destroy." 'I fear, almost, to speak, to act.'—"Happy is he that feareth always."—'I must "deny ungodliness and every worldly lust."'—"For ye are dead, and your life is hid with Christ in God." 'Having these promises, must I not cleanse myself from all "filthiness of the flesh and spirit, perfecting holiness in the fear of God?"' — "He that hath this hope in Him, purifieth himself even as He is pure."

If religion, if being a Christian, is any thing, it is every thing; it implies things of infinite importance, it involves eternal consequences. We must prize our name, our relation, as Christians, more; do more together as Christians, avail ourselves more of our Christian privileges in testimony of our obligations to Christ, and of our love to those who are partakers of like precious faith with us, through the righteousness of God and our Saviour Jesus Christ. What has Christ done for one who is a Christian? He has made him a member of his body, of his flesh, and of his bones. Not only will he be saved from endless depravity and all the miseries of hell, he will share with Christ in His future glory, — enter into the joy of his Lord. Whoever believes that this is true of him, will not fail to show it in his endeavors after perfect conformity to his Redeemer. If Christ and I are one, all that belongs to either belongs to the other. Then his cause, his people, his honor, his future glory, are mine; my soul and body, my property, my time, my talents, my influence, my joys, my afflictions and sorrows, all are his. This is literally true. Such is the perfect identification with Christ of every one who trusts in him; "for we are members of his body, of his flesh, and of his bones."

If we could practically believe this, if it would but influence our feelings and conduct, what should we need more? It would be a restraint from evil, it would impel to good; it would be a source of continual comfort and joy: great would be our faith, our hope, our peace, our love to him and to all. In believing and practising upon it, we must not be dismayed at failures, but remember that we are made members of Christ, not because we are perfectly like him, but in order that we may become so.

It is affecting and exceedingly encouraging to think that it is a very simple thing which first unites one to Christ. Here is a tree with grafted fruit. The grafted part is full, and even loaded. Once, that graft was a mere scion, but even of that, only a very small part, the edge of the bark, being brought into union with the circulation of the sap in the tree, a communication was established between the tree and the graft, and now the graft is an essential part of the tree.

One simple, heartfelt act of trust by a sinner, in Christ as an atoning Saviour, makes him one with Christ. "But the righteousness which is of faith speaketh on this wise: Say not in thine heart, who shall ascend into heaven? that is, to bring Christ down from above; or, who shall descend into the deep? that is, to bring up Christ from the dead. But what saith it? The word is nigh thee, even in thy mouth, and in thy heart; that is, the word of faith which we preach. That if thou shalt confess with thy mouth the Lord Jesus, and shalt believe in thine heart that God hath raised him from the dead, thou shalt be saved."

To be a Christian! is it repulsive to any? Does any professed Christian shrink from the obligations which a perfect identification with Christ implies? Not so will it appear to us when this Redeemer, whose members we may be, shall be seen by us as he is. Then we shall find that to be identified with Christ is the highest glory and bliss of the heavenly state. Happy, thrice happy, are all who are able to say,

" Dear Saviour, we are thine
By everlasting bonds,
Our names, our hearts, we would resign,
Our souls are in thy hands.

" To thee we still would cleave
With ever growing zeal;
If millions tempt us Christ to leave,
O let them ne'er prevail.

" Thy Spirit shall unite
Our souls to thee, our Head;
Shall form us to thy image bright,
That we thy paths may tread.

" Death may our souls divide
From these abodes of clay;
But love shall keep us near thy side,
Through all the gloomy way.

" Since Christ and we are one,
Why should we doubt and fear?
If he in heaven hath fixed his throne,
He 'll fix his members there."

DODDRIDGE.

VI.

HE SHOWED THEM HIS HANDS AND HIS FEET.

"AND WHEN HE HAD THUS SPOKEN, HE SHOWED THEM HIS HANDS AND HIS FEET."

THEY stood about him, half persuaded, yet wondering, and believing not for joy. The risen Saviour was surrounded in that upper room with his few timid disciples, kindly seeking to persuade them that it is He who was crucified and buried. He stretched forth his hands; the prints of nails driven through them were there. Those hands are like those which they had so often seen; they certainly have been nailed to a cross, and what other crucified person can it be but Jesus? His loose, upper garment plainly disclosed his feet; he bends as he stands, and directs attention to them. See that half-circle of astonished men, one or more of them holding candles as they all gaze at those feet, while the eye of the compassionate friend passes over each countenance, watching the contest of faith and fear. Those hands and feet seem to have gained the first victory, though unfinished, over their unbelief.

He was not an incorporeal spirit, but his body rose from the tomb. "He showed himself alive after his passion, by many infallible proofs." He expressly denied that He was a spirit: "Handle me, and see; for a spirit hath not flesh and bones, as ye see me have." "And he said unto them, Have ye here any meat? And they gave him a piece of a broiled fish and of an honey-comb. And he took it and did eat before them." After his resurrection from the dead, he was still, as before, God manifest in the flesh, and as such, we are expressly told, "was received up into glory." Thus, to the very moment of ascension, he had the same body as during his sojourn on earth, though its miraculous appearing and vanishing after his resurrection, lead some to think that his body had become essentially changed. It is preferable to think that, for good reasons, he forbore to use that miraculous power frequently until after his resurrection, though he evidently used it at Nazareth when they sought to cast him from the brow of the hill. His body had undergone no change in the grave; it merely came to life again, like the body of Lazarus, and like the bodies of the saints which arose at the crucifixion. During the ascension, the flesh and blood of Christ were transmuted, and his body became capable of spiritual things. But we know nothing of the chemistry of heaven, any more than of its mathematics. "He whom God raised saw no corruption." A striking phrase, describing the instantaneous change which living saints will experience at the resurrection of the dead, helps our faith with regard to the ascending body of our Lord; — "we shall not all sleep, but we shall all be changed, in a moment, in the twinkling of an eye, at the last trump." And we are expressly told that it was an exercise of omnipotence by which Christ rose and ascended: — "according to the working of his mighty power which he wrought in Christ when he raised him from the dead and set him at his own right hand in the heavenly places."

He is gone into heaven, with no change but that which we shall have, who sleep in Jesus, and the living saints who tarry till he come. Such is the testimony of those two men in white apparel: "Ye men of Gallilee, why stand ye gazing up into heaven? This same Jesus, which is taken up from you into heaven, shall so come in like manner as ye have seen him go into heaven." 'When he shall appear, we shall see him as he is.' We read that he looks like "a lamb as it had been slain." In his glorified body, then, it is supposed there will be forever something plainly visible to remind the beholder of the wounds in his hands, and feet, and side; they are his glory and joy; remembrancers to him, and to his people, and to the universe, of the cross where he was made a ransom for many. Let us think of him as having a true body as well as reasonable soul, and not only made like unto his brethren but coming to "change our vile body, that it may be fashioned like unto his glorious body, according to the working whereby he is able even to subdue all things unto himself." Now if we are to be "like him," "as he is," it is well to have just and vivid conceptions and thoughts of him, so far as Scripture leads us. What thoughts arise, therefore, as we look upon his hands and feet?

Those hands made, sustain, and govern all things. It is good if we are able unhesitatingly to say things of Christ which are true of only one of his natures, as though they belonged, as they surely do, to the inseparable oneness of his person. There is a singularly beautiful intermingling of divine and human things pertaining to Christ, in the first four verses of the Epistle to the Hebrews; — "heir of all things," — "made the worlds," — "brightness of his glory, express image of his person," — "upholding all things by the word of his power," — "purged our sins," — "made better than the angels," — "obtained a more excellent name." It is most comforting to our hearts when we can speak of an almighty, omniscient, omnipresent, and in all respects, divine Saviour, as a man, and not feel that it is inconsistent to do so. Happy are we if we can look at Christ in his manhood and say of him, — he "made the worlds;" "by him were all things created; — and he is before all things, and by him all things consist." His hands and his feet are most intimately connected with the work of our redemption.

He would not have had hands and feet but for us, and therefore, being chief executive members of the body, we may look upon them as characters which stand for the work of redemption. As when Christ showed his disciples his hands and his feet he gave them the strongest proofs that it was he, so, if we will look upon them with faith and love, we shall receive strong impressions of Christ as a personal Saviour, "bone of our bone and flesh of our flesh."

These hands and feet were once those of an infant. Immanuel, God with us, was once a young child. His mother many a time rested her forehead upon his young head, as Raphael's picture presents her to us, full of unspeakable maternal thoughts and peace. My Saviour was once as young as my own child; his hand wandered over his mother's cheek as one of his first expressions of infantile love. It is natural that parents should indulge such thoughts; and let them do it without rebuke. We have heard of a father who, having buried his infant, carried for a long time after, a little worsted shoe in his bosom, nor did any who may have listened to him as he addressed the Senate of his country, or the bench of the Supreme Court, think less of him for knowing that the little thing was at that moment hanging near his heart. Some might call it weakness, or childish, and smile at it, as we all smile at a mother's words to her infant, until, perhaps, the little child is dead, and then the man becomes a woman, and the woman oftentimes instructs and comforts the man. It is unspeakably interesting to think that my Redeemer was once a little child. The great Immanuel himself will never forget that those hands which now uphold all things by the word of his power, once could not hold even an olive-blossom, and that his feet, before which Gabriel casts his crown, followed by the crowns of heaven, once did not support his own weight. His mother, as she worships at those feet, thinks how often she spanned them and pressed them with her warm, loving palm. 'Holy child Jesus!' the apostles still loved to call thee, when Herod and Pontius Pilate and the Gentiles and the people of Israel had gathered together against thee. We look on thy hands and feet now, and we are not afraid; they were made for us, they were weak and helpless as ours were, as the hands and feet of our infants are, and as, in times of trouble, ours now are, and as in days of sickness ours will be. To those hands we commend our dying children, to those hands we intrust all that is tender and precious in our interests for this life. Nor will those feet lead us, nor our dying friends, through scenes where they themselves have not gone before.

But we must not linger here. Those hands and feet were soon, very soon about his father's business. Those feet went about doing good. Never went they into any place where he could not ask his Father's blessing. Never do we see them following after vain persons, or vain and foolish things, nor hastening with an evil report, nor to do any mischief, nor did they refuse to go anywhere and at any time, to do good. But though they walked over the tempestuous sea and trode the storm underneath them, they hastened to the bedside of the sick and dying, they stood amidst the miserable, while his hands fed them and lifted them up. They walked with Zaccheus, they went with weeping sisters to a brother's grave. They climbed the mountain, withdrew into the solitary place, where he prayed. They took him to a garden, but it was named Gethsemane, and they failed him there, under the load of our guilt. Those feet with weak, fainting, yet resolute steps came out of Jerusalem while the hands were holding upon the shoulder a cross. What were those hands and feet doing in that hour? Is it not enough to bear my sins in his own body on the tree, but will he bear the tree, also? He was willing to do that which his enemies themselves were at last unwilling to make him do, and therefore took the load from him. No wonder that the crowns of heaven are every one of them at his feet. It was his hands and feet by which he "endured the cross." Those open palms which had shed life and blessing everywhere, had each a nail driven through them; and those feet which went about doing good, were fastened among the feet of malefactors. How much was implied which was not spoken, when he stood among his disciples after he had risen, and showed them his hands and his feet. They were, and they are now, the most striking remembrancers of his sufferings.

The history of our hands and feet will be a large part of the history of our lives. The Saviour having showed us his hands and his feet at his table, we will endeavor to carry with us some impressions with regard to our duty as we come away.

We must follow his steps. We have a helpful directory to duty in this, that we may always ask, How would Christ decide and act in this case? We may not go where we cannot suppose his footsteps might not be, nor where we cannot take him with us, nor where we cannot implore his blessing. How many steps we shall have taken when we go to his table again! how many places we shall visit, unknown and unsuspected now, but they will be safe places if we but set him before us. "In all thy ways acknowledge him, and he shall direct thy paths." Our feet will not carry us with bad company, if we think of the feet of Christ; nor to spread an evil report against our neighbor; nor to do any mischief, nor will they profane the Sabbath, nor refuse, for insufficient reasons, to visit the house of God and the prayer-meeting; nor will they move in wanton dances, nor stand in the way of sinners. What errands of love and mercy they may perform; how like the steps of angels they will be if we keep our eye on the feet of Christ. Perhaps they will travel to far distant places, and stand on foreign soil. "He will not suffer thy foot to be moved; he that keepeth thee will not slumber." Our feet may bear us to the grave of one whom we love; it may be said of you as of him: "Then cometh he to a place which is called Gethsemane." Forerunner! we cannot follow thee to such an experience as that of the garden and the cross, however bitter and dreadful our sufferings may be. Sickness may disable us, and our feet be placed, as it were, in the stocks. They cannot be nailed to the cross, and in all things we may be more than conquerors through him that loved us. If we walk at liberty in our daily business, we must consecrate all we do to him who gives us the power to get wealth. Some who go to his table to-day will tread the paths of learning. Perhaps some who read these words are this day to join the church of Christ. The history of those feet which are thus to tread the aisles of the sanctuary to-day, binding the sacrifice with cords even to the horns of the altar, what a history it may be and will be, if they but mark the footsteps of Christ. It may be said of some of them by grateful nations, How beautiful upon the mountains are the feet of him that bringeth good tidings; that publisheth peace, that bringeth good tidings of good, that publisheth salvation; that saith unto Zion, Thy God reigneth. No more will those feet go away from the table of Christ, Sabbath after

Sabbath, but, "until he come," they are to bring you into the circle of his friends, to sit with him at his table. Let your consecration be without any reserve. Say, "Lord, not my feet only, but also my hands and my head."

And shall these hands, which join with Christ's hands in this covenant to-day, have a history this coming month or months, inconsistent with such vows, such blessings? These hands which take the body and blood of Christ, how holy they ought to be. They shall not withhold any thing from Christ which he requires of us, nor be shut against the needy; they shall work no ill to a neighbor, keep back no just due; they shall be diligent in business, as the hands of Christ must have been when he worked at his trade and dignified our labor; they shall strike no passionate blow; they shall use severity at proper times, sustained by divine authority; they shall shed kindness and blessings on others; they shall write no letters which the eye of Christ might not be permitted to read; they shall receive no gains on which we cannot ask his blessing. May we be .able, at the next communion season, to show Christ our hands and our feet with joy and peace, as he now shows us his. These hands may be full of prosperity in business; they may give and receive the grasp of new friendships and love; some of them may be given in marriage; they may receive from God the richest blessing ever laid in them. All these things, be it remembered, will have been purchased for us by those hands which were nailed to the tree. And some of these hands, now united in love, may be unclasped by death, be folded upon the bosom for the long sleep, and, as they brought nothing into the world, carry nothing out. But when the hand of earthly love lets go its hold, there is a hand that will clasp ours which will be far better. Therefore, while Christ to-day shows us his hands and his feet, let us show him ours, "a living sacrifice, which is your reasonable service."

There is a time approaching when, not by faith, but with our eyes, we shall together look upon those hands and feet. Those hands will separate many, one from another. By one or the other of those hands, each of us will be welcomed, or bid to depart. Christ did not hang by one hand only, and that his right hand, upon the cross. That left hand was also nailed there; and shall I see it consign me to my doom? I must not, need not, shall not, if I now commit my soul to his hands. Otherwise, with its print of the nail, it will point me to my doom.

Let each one who reads these words and is not a communicant, give himself to Christ in sight of his table this day, remaining there as a spectator. If one should remain, it may lead others to do so. How we wait for one another in coming to Christ, but outrun others in getting the world. Let your feet lead you to a seat where you may witness the Lord's Supper, and while your hands seek, perhaps, to hide your feelings, you may have covenant transactions with Christ. Be a Christian to-day. By the wounded hands and feet of Christ, be not ashamed of him, but begin to love him and to confess him before men. When all enemies are under his feet, and his hands have divided our last rewards, you may remember this communion Sabbath, as the beginning of communion and fellowship with Christ without end.

VII.

COMMUNION WITH CHRIST.

"The cup of blessing which we bless, is it not the communion of the blood of Christ? The bread which we break, is it not the communion of the body of Christ?"

In celebrating the Passover, before the singing of the hymn, a cup was distributed among the company at the close of the feast, and was therefore called the cup of benediction, or blessing. It was this cup with which Christ instituted the Ordinance of the Lord's Supper, as Luke informs us in these words: "Likewise also the cup after supper," (that is, the Passover Supper,) "saying, This cup is the New Testament in my blood which is shed for you."

The Saviour sat down to eat the Passover, and changed it into the Lord's Supper, converting the national ordinance into the great, commemorative rite of his future church, thus quietly joining the two dispensations of Moses and the Lamb into one, as from the beginning they were the same. So that there is an original congruity between the Passover and the Lord's Supper, which we are also taught when we read that 'Christ our passover is sacrificed for us.' The Sabbath of creation goes, peaceful as sunrise, into the Lord's day; and, in like manner, as the old, waning moon, which we see, for some time, after daylight, at last takes her place, a beautiful crescent, in the west, so the Passover waned and, still true to its name, passes over to another shape and rules in our sky, till the day break and the shadows flee away.

'The cup which we bless,' or consecrate, was originally a token of special communion and love in a transaction the whole of which commemorated the love of God, in a most deeply interesting crisis of his people's history. We, then, may look upon the cup, before we receive it, as a gracious benediction, and be prepared to find in its intended use nothing but loving-kindness. The cup which we bless, let it be observed in passing, derives no virtue from any ministerial act; for ministers do not alone bless the cup; all who pray with them, bless it, that is, hallow it, set it apart from a common to a sacramental use. Each communicant, therefore, equally with the rest and with the officiating minister, blesses the cup by uniting in the prayer of consecration.

"Is it not the communion of the blood of Christ?" Suppose that it were literally blood. It could not be any more significant than the cup now is intended to be. To repeat an illustration in a previous part of this book, money is given and received when, instead of coin, a paper representative, duly authorized, is employed.

It is then, the communion, the participating, of the blood of Christ, which takes place when we give and receive the cup. If so, we do great injustice to the Saviour's design, indeed it is almost a perversion of it, when we invest it with a forbidding, terrific character. It is possible so to represent the Lord's Supper that men will regard it very much with the feelings of Moses when he said, I do exceedingly fear and quake. Indeed, the fear of violating the sacredness of the ordinance is, with conscientious people, unsurpassed by any dread whatever, especially when they connect with it the remembrance of those fearful words, "eateth and drinketh damnation to himself" by eating and drinking unworthily. Explanations and reasonings do but little with such persons. We tell them, almost in vain, that, by their interpretation of those words, it must follow that every one who partakes of the Lord's Supper and is convinced afterwards that he was not then converted, is made thereby a subject of hopeless damnation,— which, of course, they see to be absurd, knowing how many have truly embraced Christ, for the first time, after they had, through mistake and by undue persuasion, made a profession of their faith. The solemn admonition of the Apostle to those Corinthians who turned the Lord's Supper into ordinary feasting, and behaved in a rude and gluttonous way which seems to us incredible, is, of course, applicable to all who do not care to 'discern' any difference between partaking of the Lord's body, and of an ordinary meal. Never, surely, was it designed to repel from the ordinance any, whose conscientious fears of intrusion make them exactly the opposites of the inconsiderate persons to whom the Apostle addressed himself.

Now the way to encourage ourselves in approaching this ordinance, is not to make it less sacred and solemn in our estimation, but to consider the way, for there is a way, in which, sacred and solemn as it is, we may be included in that affectionate appeal of the Saviour, "Drink ye all of it." Surely, if this blood was shed for the remission of sins, it is not with a stern heart, nor a cold face, nor a hesitating hand that Christ invites us to this supper.

Among those in whom pastors have confidence that they are sincere followers of Christ, there is occasionally one who complains that the Lord's Supper does not afford that degree of comfort which is desired, and such as others seem to experience.

There are others who would be glad to be released from the obligation to attend upon the ordinance, persuaded, as they are, that they were never born of the Spirit.

Are there not, also, some who live in known sin, yet feel obliged to be at the Lord's Supper either as a duty which they fear to neglect, or as a means of concealing their sin, which, if they absented themselves, would be suspected ?

To these last, every thing may be said which would be appropriate as a reproof for neglecting secret prayer and religion in general; and beside that, by the more special profession of approach to Christ at his table, and by receiving from him the peculiar tokens of his love, they become hardened in sin and make themselves liable to present and future judgments.

In warning them, and repeating to them the threatenings of God, we almost always terrify and distress one of the other classes who are persuaded that they have no right to sit at the table, because they have no hope that they were truly converted. Still their desire is to be sincere, and nothing pains them so much as the absence of satisfying proof that they are accepted of Christ.

Between these, and reprobates, there is the difference which was once illustrated in a coarse manner, yet with great truth, through a figure which being rendered in other terms, is to this effect. The difference between a reprobate and a sincere, though doubting, and even despairing, Christian, is the same as we see in a wicked man who is cast out of a church, and a member who is excommunicated for some grievous offence and yet is at heart a Christian. The two are like different classes of animals when excluded from the sheepfold. The swine seeks the pools of water and the mire, rejoicing in his liberty; the sheep, driven out, bleats around the fold, or, if she wanders a while, returns, and shows that her heart is still in the fold. So, the sorrow and pain which some of our communicants feel at the want of comfortable evidence that they are accepted of Christ, is sufficient proof that they belong to his true flock. There is no better test of piety than our desires. The Psalms of David afford as much proof of his being a child of God, when he laments the absence of religious comforts, as when he exults with his harp; indeed, religious joy is more liable to be deceptive than religious sorrow.

The first class which we referred to, have suggested the remarks which follow; — they complain that they do not derive that satisfying enjoyment from the Lord's Supper as an ordinance which they desire and might expect.

The reason of this has been found, in several cases, to be, that the individuals expected impressions to be made upon their minds, responses, as it were, from Christ, assurances that he heard and regarded them; for such things they understand to be communion with Christ.

They do not sufficiently consider the difference between hope and faith. To pray, to perform every religious duty, with the firm persuasion that God hears, and will, in his own time and way, answer, but to require no sensible impressions upon the mind at the time, in reply, is to ask in faith. But, to make our comfort and the performance of our duty depend on the response which we may seem to receive, is not the highest exercise of love to God or trust in him. Communion with Christ does not require responsive influences upon our hearts in order to be real. This, and other things relating to a proper understanding of the subject, may appear in the sequel.

In partaking of the body and blood of Christ, we should be persuaded of his infinite love to us. This feeling ought to prevail over every other. It should lead our thoughts, constitute the atmosphere around the table; for this seems not only to be suggested, but to be required, by the words of Christ, in appointing the ordinance, "This do in remembrance of me." For we never ask any one to remember us but with a feeling of love. Remember me! there is always gentleness, pathos, seeming entreaty, in such words. They imply need; they are the words of the parting friend, the absent friend, the dying friend. Remember me! Can coldness, or repulsiveness, or suspicion, or jealousy, live in the heart which feels and utters such a wish, such a request? Surely, then, if the cup which we bless is the communion, or participation, of the blood of Christ shed for us, and now by his own hand offered to us, reciprocal love and confidence on our part toward him should be our ruling emotion. By what means could he persuade us, if not by the communion of his body and blood, that he loves us and seeks our love? Therefore to every one who shrinks from this solemn act with a sense of his own unworthiness, forgetting the righteousness of Christ which is placed to the believing sinner's account, and fears, lest the breaking of the bread may be to him as when the Lamb opened one of the seals, and there were lightnings, and thunderings, and voices, we may speak in the Saviour's name, and remonstrate, saying, "The cup of blessing which we bless, is it not the communion of the blood of Christ? The bread which we break, is it not the communion of the body of Christ?"

But what relation do that body and blood have to me? — The Redeemer stands at the first sacramental table, and says, "This is my body which is broken for you; this cup is the New Testament in my blood which is shed for you." Instead of being repelled by it, what is there, in heaven or in earth, which should draw us with such cords of love, or inspire us with such confidence?

You are dangerously sick, and the attendant holds forth to you a medicine which has cured many who were as sick as you. In prison, doomed for life, a redeemer comes to you with the bills of exchange which have been negotiated for your ransom. You might as properly shrink from the sight of that remedy and of that ransom, as from the table of Christ. Here is the balm from Gilead, and the physician with it; here is the Redeemer, and for you he has found a ransom.

True it is that there must be reciprocation on our part; we do not passively receive the communion, as a helpless creature receives extreme unction; the bread and the wine are helpers of our faith and love; there must be communion with Christ if the ordinance is understood and properly received.

But what is communion with Christ? If we can arrive at just ideas upon this subject it will be of great practical use.

Communion with Christ implies a likeness of views and feelings. Friends cannot be said to have communion of spirit unless they concur in things which deeply interest them, and take essentially the same views of the most important things. Separations between friends, not unfrequently, take place because they differ with regard to some subject which deeply interested both parties, or one of them is absorbed in a thing which gives the other no pleasure. Communion with Christ implies that the things which chiefly interest him, interest us, that we take substantially the same views of things as to their relative importance.

The supreme motive of Christ, David thus expressed: "I delight to do thy will, O my God; yea, thy law is within my heart." The obedience and conformity of men to God, was the end for which he lived and died. His primary object was not to bring us off from punishment, but to restore to God his revolted subjects; and all his exhortations, the words of counsel and direction with which he inspired his Apostles to teach us, have this for their great end, to make us good; not happy, as the first object, but as a consequence of knowing and doing our duty. That compassion is not the fundamental principle of his character and conduct, but the love of holiness, we learn when it is said, that "the Son of man shall send forth his angels and they shall gather out of his kingdom all things which offend and them which do iniquity, and shall cast them into a furnace of fire; there shall be wailing and gnashing of teeth." And at the last day, he who died for all, and would have all men to be saved, and was able to save them to the uttermost, will nevertheless say to a multitude for whom he died, "Depart from me, ye cursed." The interests of holiness, the honor of God, are the great concern with Christ. Every thing conspires to make us know and feel this. We submit to God when we come into his kingdom; own his justice; yield to his disposal; exalt Him and abase ourselves. It is the first and essential effect of atonement, in our souls, to set up the authority of God there, and to change us from disobedient, to the obedient children of God.

Therefore to have communion with Christ, we must enter into the great purpose of his coming, his death, resurrection, and mediatorial reign. The authority and the glory of God must stand in our view as it did in the view of the Saviour, as the great end for which we exist, and ought ever to live, saying, "For thy pleasure we are, and were created." Those prayers of Christ which breathe such a spirit of love to God and confidence in Him, such submission and joy in view of his will, must find an approval in our breasts.

It is in vain that we expect communion with Christ as a friend and Saviour unless it is based on this agreement between us. Every thing without this, however melting, or rapturous, or in any way emotional, is imaginative and deceptive. "If ye had known me, ye should have known my father also." While this is admonitory, is it not also encouraging? It shows religion, in its highest exercises and attainments, to be based on correct views of things, a right understanding, and not on fancy, which is not subject to our volitions, and is a faculty which in many is deficient; while correct knowledge and obedience to the truth are within the reach of all who are willing to hear and receive instruction.

Having seen to it that our hearts are right with him as to the ruling motive and the fundamental principle of our views and feelings, our object will properly be to ascertain in what way Christ, and the soul of one who thus agrees with him, have communion by means of his ordinance of the Supper.

Communion with Christ takes place when we have intercourse with him by faith. This is true of communion in prayer, and it is the same, of course, at the table, where our minds are more forcibly impressed, by the sight of his appointed memorials of his own body and blood. When it is said, 'He that cometh to God must believe that he is,' a mere conviction of his existence is not meant, but, a practical conviction that he is cognizant of our prayer, to believe which is to be persuaded of his omnipresence and omniscience; "that he is" there, where we pray, and is a rewarder of them that diligently seek him. Applying this to Christ, we must believe that he listens to what we say to him in the secrecy of our thoughts, and if we believe any thing aright concerning Christ, we must believe this. Our danger and our great error will consist in thinking that we must receive from him any impressive signs that he listens and responds to us. We must not require nor expect this. We must perform our part of the communion by expressing to him our thoughts and feelings, and leaving the rest to him.

His methods of communing with us will be various. Some who complain that they do not have it, are mistaken. They express to him feelings of deep interest to them, with confessions, and penitence, and a consciousness of entire reliance upon him, a dread of sin, fear of the future, resignation of themselves to his hands, and they do not consider that it is he who has inspired them with these feelings and thus answered their prayers. Strong impressions of his personal access to them they may not have, and these are not essential to communion with him. We have communion with Christ when we impart to him, as personally present with us, our thoughts and feelings. But as the greatest favor which he can give us is, not rapture, nor any form or degree of joy, but to increase our faith, he may withhold from us any sense of his nearness to us, and yet make us feel and act as though we saw or heard him at our side. When we can do this, we rise to a high exercise of faith. The more we are able to do this, the safer will our religious experience be, less fanciful, more uniform, for then it will not depend on frames of mind, or moods of feeling.

Let us fully believe, then, at the table of Christ, as well as elsewhere, but especially at the place which he has appointed for particular communion with him, that he is at our side. We do not need to ask as a disciple did, 'Lord, how is it that thou wilt manifest thyself unto us, and not unto the world.' This disciple wondered how Christ could conceal himself from the rest of the world upon his promised return, and confine himself to the company of the disciples. But on answering this question, so perfectly natural in the imperfect state of information which the disciples had respecting the Saviour's future history, Christ discloses a truth to him which corrected his misapprehension and imparted a joyful assurance to all his friends. "Jesus saith unto him, If a man love me, he will keep my words, and my father will love him, and we will come unto him and make our abode with him." We are told who put the question which called forth this answer: "Judas saith unto him, (not Iscariot.)" We thank thee, Evangelist, for this information; yet we would have suspected that such a question would not have issued from Iscariot. Little did he care how Christ would manifest himself to him, or that he should do it at all. The answer, too, was one which it required a mind predisposed at least to spiritual impressions to appreciate and remember.

It is the chief privilege and benefit at the Lord's Supper to have personal communion with Christ. Never may we in this world come near to him with greater encouragement or help to our weak faith than when we sit at his table. We eat of his body, we drink of his blood; will he invite, will he command us to do this, and he be wanting in his part of the communion? for bread, will he give us a stone? We should not call our children to our table, for communion with us, and fail to regard their wishes. He will choose his own best way of promoting our fellowship with him, but he will not be wanting on his part. For, communion implies more than one.

Suppose that we anticipate this ordinance, as we do a meeting with some very dear friend; that we prepare for it, that we consider beforehand what we will say to Christ when he is at our side, during the supper, what confessions, what temptations, what trials, what requests, what praises and thanksgivings we will make known to him, and what exercises of repentance, faith, love, humility, forgiveness, contentment, hope, submission, we will desire to have while he is with us; what thoughts of heaven, what fears of dying, what prayers for his special presence in any expected hour of need, we will express. Suppose that we talk with him as with the best friend, compared with whom an earthly friend, a lover, even, is a poor, helpless worm; and that we seal our covenant to be his with his precious blood, and by eating of his body broken for us, — this, this, will indeed be communion, such as no other place, or scene of worship, affords, or is intended to afford. This does not make it necessary that we imagine his looks, or that we see him hanging on the cross, or making any sign to us. "For we walk by faith, not by sight." We cannot, however, do this, habitually, and not experience the fulfilment of the Saviour's promise, "we will come unto him and make our abode with him."

A proof that we have done this, and experienced the fruit of it, will appear by this additional evidence of habitual communion and fellowship with Christ, that we espouse the things which are dear to him.

This is a peculiarity of love, that every-thing which interests the beloved object, interests us. His friendships, his hatreds, especially his endeavors to promote his own interests, to vindicate himself, or to effect a desired object, moves our affections, and we identify ourselves with them. So that if we have communion with Christ, we shall be identified, increasingly, in our feelings, with those things for which the Saviour laid down his life.

But there are some who, while they seem to be in the family of Christ, have only that relation to it which transient inmates have to a family. In some households, there are those who are with the family only at meal time. They sustain, it is true, a pleasant, friendly relation to the family; but they are not of the family. The intimacies of family communion, the secrets of love, and joy, and sorrow, of prosperity and disappointment, the hearing the letter from the absent child or parent, the consultations about the interests of the family, — they are not admitted to these things. So, we may be only occupants of seats at Christ's board, always present, indeed, at meal time; but where are we, and what are we, at other times? Christ's family have family meetings, other meetings than those at his table and to receive food in his house, meetings of very near and dear fellowship, where plans for promoting the welfare of the family and the honor of the divine Head are considered, and where He comes in, the doors being shut, and says, Peace be unto you.

"There would I find a settled rest
While others go and come;
No more a stranger, or a guest,
But like a child at home."

Do we know any thing of this? Or are we mere table companions of Christ? If so, it would be strange if we did not complain of not having enjoyment at the Lord's Supper, and did not know what communion with Christ means. Or if we professed to have enjoyment there, it would be suspicious. Do we expect to go from a life of worldliness and sin to a peaceful, happy dying bed, or, having been indifferent to the interests of Christ's kingdom on earth, do we think that an entrance will be ministered unto us abundantly into the everlasting kingdom of our Lord and Saviour Jesus Christ? No more can we expect communion with Christ at his table unless we lead religious lives. The exercises of mind at the Lord's table, are the ordinary exercises of a Christian, promoted to greater measures by the peculiar means appointed there to affect our hearts.

VIII.

SALUTATIONS AT THE SEPULCHRE.

"JESUS SAITH UNTO HER, MARY! SHE TURNED HERSELF AND SAITH UNTO HIM, RABBONI! WHICH IS TO SAY, MASTER!"

THERE were, thus far, only two words spoken, in this conversation, all the rest being the explanatory words of the historian. The two words which were spoken, and which constituted the salutations at the sepulchre, were these: "Mary!" "Master!" But what a dialogue! The heart and tongue of John were necessary fully to unfold the beauty and power of these words.

They remind us of those household salutations which contain so much. The love born and nourished at home, finds some of its best utterances in sudden greetings. As you meet unexpectedly at the doors, or upon the stairs, coming in, going out, or by the way, one word, perhaps, is uttered, the hallowed name of father, mother, the child's name, the words of intenser love than husband, or wife, yet synonymous with them, the half playful brotherly or sisterly appellation, or the gush of love at the sight of the youngest born. All that is blissful in human love sometimes finds expression in the simple, sudden utterance of one of these names.

He who added to his divine nature a heart of exquisite mould, possessed, and could appreciate every thing which enters into the nature of human love. He had first awakened the attention of this weeper at the sepulchre, and yet her thoughts were so enchained to that vacant spot where Jesus slept, that she did not turn herself at the question of sympathy, Woman, why weepest thou? which the supposed gardener was speaking to her. Then the charmed word was uttered, and awoke her from the spell which the grave had laid upon her sorrowful spirit.

Who is this that calls her familiarly by name! This is some other than the gardener. There is a tone of acquaintance and love in the utterance. "Mary!" who can express all that might have entered into her heart in that one moment, conveyed by that name from those lips!

It was the salutation of a friend returning unawares. He stood before her alive. She was searching for his remains. All her desire was expressed in those words, Sir, if thou have borne him hence, tell me where thou hast laid him, and I will take him away. Not thirty-six hours before, the crucifixion had taken place, and from the anguish of that scene this loving heart had not yet gained relief, but on the contrary, was experiencing new pangs on missing the form she loved so well. All the dark and sorrowful past was filled with new dismay, its heavy clouds seemed agitated by a rising wind which was mixing every thing in worse confusion; the dreadful death was now followed by a rifled grave, the separation was deprived of that poor solace, to weep over the precious dust. In such circumstances, perhaps we can imagine what that one word must have been to her: "Mary!" The voice she knew, and in that moment a great stone was rolled away from her heart.

The first address calling her attention was by the name, Woman. All the Saviour's compassion and kindness to her in times past and in that moment, found utterance in a second word. His heart was touched by the proof she was even then giving him of a love stronger than death, watching at his deserted tomb, fixing her gaze upon that spot where he last disappeared from her view, and so entranced by its power over her that she replies to a voice of sympathy and kind inquiry behind her, without at this time turning herself from her look into the sepulchre. Such affecting love must have touched the heart of Christ, such fidelity, such undying attachment, must have infused unwonted feeling into the expression of her name. It had in it the joyfulness which love feels in knowing the glad surprise which it has in its power to impart, and so partook of the bliss which it was itself to awaken in the heart of the disconsolate friend.

The disciples once saw that same form in the fourth watch of the night walking upon the sea, and they cried out for fear. Thinking only of her buried friend, and of his lifeless remains borne thence, she knew not whether by friendly or unfriendly hands, her thoughts absorbed in efforts to find the inanimate clay, the sudden appearance of Jesus to her, alive, we would suppose, must have overpowered her senses; but the kindness which flowed toward her in the use of her familiar name, kept back the tide of feeling, otherwise too great for nature, from overpowering her heart. "Master!" was there ever a word that conveyed a greater combination of feelings wrought to a higher pitch? Conviction seems to have been instantaneous. The heart of Thomas was not in her. Faith, which had not been clouded even by sorrows, was in a moment changed for sight. Jesus had undergone no change in death and the resurrection; his voice, and then one glance at him, called up his wonted name. Some heavenly artist alone might truly sketch the look, the motions, the whole expression of that scene on either side; it was a scene such as earth had seldom witnessed; and yet in all which gave it real value, it may be repeated in the experience of believers.

For, who needs to be told of the power which there oftentimes is in one word of Christ to a sorrowful spirit? All that Jesus needed to say to his weeping friend was, "Mary;" then did her light rise in obscurity, and her darkness was as the noonday. So has a sin-stricken soul, laboring and heavy laden, seeking Christ, weeping and casting itself on him, suddenly felt that Christ had spoken one word of peace to it, and the day-star rose in the heart. It was but a word, "be of good cheer," "fear not," "only believe," or something, which, heard before a thousand times in vain, now spoken to a waiting and trustful heart, becomes like the word which chaos heard, and there was light; which death and the grave hear and obey. A life of guilt, a sense of the wrath of God, despair of ever being under any law but that of evil, has yielded to the word of Christ, and there was a great calm. Among the experiences of weeping, broken spirits, few are sweeter and richer than the sense of perfect ease with which a work is done at once which years had not accomplished. Such was the effect of the Saviour's word to the leper, "I will, be thou clean;" and to the blind eyes, "Be opened," and to the widow's son, "Arise;" and to the weeping penitent, "Thy sins are forgiven thee; go in peace." One word of Christ has full power to effect every thing which we need. We must believe this, and not limit that power by magnifying the difficulties of our case.

There is no more striking exercise of almighty goodness than that strength of heart which is sometimes imparted to us in trouble. None of the circumstances are changed; but God has suddenly raised our spirits, unwonted hope has taken possession of us. Some coincidence, some noticeable event, occurring in singular connection with our thoughts and prayers, suddenly inspires us with all the effect of revelation. The watcher, looking out upon the sky and not suspecting dawn, is suddenly cheered by a sign of day.

> "So fairest Phosphor, the bright morning star,
> But newly washed in the green element, —
> Before the drowsy night is half aware,
> Springs lively up into th' orient."

Every thing seems changed, and it is because of some new turn in affairs, some kind message, some friendly word of cheer, some discovery of help and relief, a fear disappointed, a lost expectation coming back fulfilled. What power God has to help us wonderfully by little things, and sometimes without the aid of any thing external. "In the multitude of my thoughts within me, thy comforts delight my soul."

The name of every believer is dear to Christ. "He calleth his own sheep by name and leadeth them out." Think of some of the times and ways in which you have seemed to hear, and may yet hear, Christ speaking to you by name. It may be that you are oppressed with a sense of unworthiness, and feel that no one is interested in you, or loves you. There is one who loved you in foresight of all your unworthiness, and himself bare your sins in his own body on the tree. His love is not fluctuating, like yours. "Having loved his own which were in the world, he loved them unto the end." Nothing can divide us from him. "Who shall separate us from the love of Christ." Difficulties which appall us do not move him. "He fainteth not neither is weary." As you sit alone, oppressed with grief, he seems to speak your name, and addresses you. It is a familiar name to him; he read it in the book of life, before the world was; he has read it times without number; it is one of the essential records in that book of life; humble, and a worthless name, as you esteem it, this is the Father's will that of all that he has given him, he should lose nothing. To the man, he says, "my son;" but of her who retains her Christian name with those who have grown up with her, or have come to love her, and of every child, the Christian name is familiar, and in speaking to them, he would use that name. "Mary" shall lend us her name for illustration.

Trouble and anguish have come upon you; bereavement, calamity, a crushing load. He foresaw the whole, he designed it, he knew what it would be; the furnace of affliction was prepared by him, and "lo!" said the king of Babylon, 'I see four men walking in the midst of the fire, and the form of the fourth is like the Son of God.' We do not read of Christ calling Judas by name; but he said, "Simon, Simon," and "Thou art Peter," and, "Be of good cheer, Paul." Should you but hear him speak your name to you, all would be well. Faith may hear it. "I have called thee by thy name; thou art mine."

You are anticipating an hour of suffering. Nature faints at it. Life and death seem hung in even scales. Momentous is to be the issue of that expected hour, and Jesus knows it. All that is delicate and hidden in your condition, he knows; 'and underneath are the everlasting arms.' One word, "Mary!" from him, will be enough. Put your hand in his. You can go through any thing if he but speak your name to you, now and then, with a look of love. He will speak that name. "When thou passest through the waters I will be with thee, and through the rivers they shall not overflow thee." Let come what will, "his loving-kindness is better than life."

The coming month you are expecting an event which is to have an important, it may be an all important, bearing upon your whole future life. Some child, or near and dear friend, in whom you are bound up, may be in this condition. You are going to the Lord's table to-day. He that sat on the well when a woman came thither to draw, and uttered to her some of the most important truths of his ministry, and, we trust, saved her soul, but, more particularly, he whose very first words, so far as we are informed, with which he broke the silence of the tomb, were, "Woman, why weepest thou?" expects you. It will be a favor to you, and to very many like you, we know not how many, perhaps all, if we, ministers, who conduct the service at the table, refrain from much speaking, especially on controverted or agitating subjects, and from common-place remarks, and when we have sent forth the bread and the cup to you, if we will be still, and 'let' your 'religious hours alone.' For you are ready to finish the quotation: —

> "Fain would my eyes my Saviour see,
> I wait a visit, Lord, from thee."

Commune with him respecting this great event; think of him as he himself was passing through critical seasons of his earthly life; call him "forerunner," "shepherd," "Captain;" "my refuge and my fortress; my God, in him will I trust." Receive his body and blood, all which it was possible for him to give you, (or he would have given you more,) and while he pledges himself to you in this way, give over to him all your precious interests, and make a covenant with him by sacrifice. O hallowed, heavenly moments! What a sight is a communing church, their heads bowed low in converse with Christ. What a being Christ is, Immanuel, God with us, at the side of every one of those dear saints of his, and at the minister's side, and with each beloved church officer who bears the vessels of the Lord.

What a season must communion seasons be to Christ. Bethlehem! Gethsemane! Calvary! Olivet! these are rivals with you in the Saviour's interest, when his saints commune with him over his body and blood. The little church of converted Aborigines with their faithful, loving teachers, the church in the greater wilderness of heathenism and paganism beyond sea, the church of emigrants with household utensils for flagons and cups, the ship's company in mid ocean, the dying saint and the two or three who are gathered together at the bedside, and the great missionary convocation representing as nearly as possible the kindreds of the earth, are scenes to Christ in which he begins to see of the travail of his soul and to be satisfied. The crown of the whole is, that to each he says, "Mary!" and that every Mary can, with truth, say, "This is my beloved, and this is my friend."

Perhaps you need to come, and are coming, to the table, as one who has very much to confess, and to be forgiven. The annunciation and approach of the Communion Sabbath may have arrested and awakened you in sin, or forgetfulness, or in some departure from God. You may have grown cold and careless. Pleasure may have enticed you, some earthly love may have beguiled you. How has it been with your Bible, and prayer? We are told that at one of the missionary schools in the East, the praying girls at one time had each her retreat for prayer in the jungle hard by, to which the trodden grass pointed the way, but when she had become prayerless, it passed into a proverb: Her path to the bush is grown over. How is this with you? If you have wandered, be not dismayed. One office of Christ as Shepherd is thus expressed: "He restoreth my soul." In its connection, it is affecting to read the last verse of the one hundred and nineteenth Psalm, and to think that a man who had made that record of religious experience and piety, should find it necessary to close all by saying, "I have gone astray like a lost sheep; seek thy servant, for I do not forget thy commandments." Let us have hope.

Are you on a journey? are you in the midst of fashion, at places where the gay world has her throne? Jesus comes and stands in the midst, and says "Mary!" How does his voice sound there? Little cares he for that intoxicating show of splendor and fashion, and all the luxurious feelings which make revel there; he comes because one for whom he died and intercedes, is there, and into that wilderness of spiritual things, perhaps he comes to find the sheep which he had lost. Is his voice welcome? When he says "Mary!" do you gladly answer, "Master!" Or is your name upon his lips in such a place, like the look which he turned and gave to Peter; and would your name spoken there, or anywhere, by Jesus, make you go out and weep bitterly?

You are engaged in some self-denying or dutiful act

of love to an aged, or sick, or poor relative, or friend, or stranger. Perhaps your companions are following their innocent or their delirious pleasures, and have left you alone with your duty and your reflections. Jesus is there; and, out of heaven, is there a moment of peace surpassing that when, with approving look and tone, he says to you, "Mary!" At such a moment, what is the whole world to you?

Now you are disappointed in something on which you had set your heart. It seems that the whole of life now will be a different thing, a gloomy thing, because of that loss. Your sun, you say, is gone down while it is yet noon.

But there is one who openeth and no man shutteth. He meets you amidst the wreck and ruin of your hopes. Perhaps your feelings are agonized. Tears are your meat day and night. Inexpressibly bitter is the cup which you take with you into your solitude to drink. There is one who took from the same hand a cup far more bitter. You have found, you think, your Gethsemane, but Gethsemane forbids that the same name be applied to any scene of trial which comes to us; trial, too, which is to be for good to them that love God. Remembering Gethsemane, he says to you, "Mary!" 'Can you drink of the cup that I drink of?' Will you have fellowship with me in my sufferings? These trials are a part of redeeming mercy, and that ingredient in the cup which makes it revolting, serves to make it efficacious. If he, the man of sorrows, but speak your name to you in the greatest affliction, it is enough. He remembers you. 'The Lord thinketh upon me.' All is well.

Now we see you at the grave's side, sorrowing over that mound, or at the door of that tomb which has changed the world for you into a vale of tears. There comes one as you are bowed down with grief, and he needs but to say, "Mary!" and what then? The Resurrection and the Life bears your name upon his lips, and upon his heart, and it is graven on his hands. These words of Jesus which, it has already been observed, were the first after the resurrection of which we have any knowledge, "Woman, why weepest thou? whom seekest thou?" were uttered before a tomb. What if your dead should appear to you in celestial beauty, and, side by side, Jesus should also appear? To which of them would you first draw nigh? At whose feet would you fall? Instantly you would feel the infinite superiority of your God and Saviour to a mere worm, however endeared and however longed for. While you are weeping at the grave, therefore, know that a voice is speaking to you far more to be desired than that of the loved and lost friend or child. "I am the first and the last." Make the grave the place to enthrone Christ in your heart, and his love and sympathy will help you to enjoy safely the luxury of grief; for there is luxury in grief. You may carry your sorrow with you as long as you live; but as the moisture of the climate around the British isles clothes England with a peculiar verdure, so the constant presence of a sanctified grief makes the heart and mind like a green meadow, opens it to the richest influences, and renders it prolific. Let the risen Saviour but speak your name occasionally to the ear of your faith alone, and you will go in the strength of it many days.

There is a watch word for us in Mary's salutation: "Master!" — "Ye call me Master, and Lord, and ye say well; for so I am." That word must be the expression of the heartfelt love of which obedience is the best, indeed the only sure, sign. He speaks to us, disinclined to duty, shrinking from sacrifice and suffering, from death, affliction, protracted grief. He calls us, and points to the dark, or the thorny, or the narrow way. "Master!" our response must be. He requires of us the surrender of something dear to us; calls for aid to his cause, levies contribution upon his own which he has given us; and can we say, — do we say, from the heart, "Master!" We are not our own; we are bought with a price; what is our ruling motive? what is our end in life? do we look upon our own things, or upon the things which are Jesus Christ's? Could it take a bodily form, what passion, what pursuit, what desire, what employment should we look upon and say, "Master!" "One is your Master, even

Christ." Do you know him by that name? or only as Saviour? "He is thy Lord; and worship thou him." For, "What offices does Christ execute, as our Redeemer?"

If we do this as the habit of our lives, there will be times when at sudden and great mercies and blessings, temporal and spiritual, he will make us exclaim, as Mary did, "Master!" Mary's exclamation was one of joy. So will ours frequently be, for his divine power has given unto us all things pertaining to life and godliness, and among them exceeding great and precious promises, the fulfilment of which, beautiful in their season, will be to us like the discoveries of new and wonderful features of scenery in a journey through a land of mountains and streams.

There is a time coming when these salutations at the Sepulchre will literally be exchanged between Christ and you. Three times in one discourse the Saviour says of every one that believes in him, "And I will raise him up at the last day." Standing at your sepulchre, clothed with your new body like unto Christ's own glorious body, the joy of your heart will rise higher than ever when the Saviour, contemplating your perfect beauty, his own gift, and rejoicing with you in it, comes and says to you, "Mary!" Then, with emotions which will be heaven begun, and with large advances of its joy, you will see the King in his beauty, and, O word of rapture, spoken then with new meaning, you will say "Master!" You who have followed him here in the straight and narrow way, in darkness, in lengthening shadows and sorrows, and to many a grave, will then turn and follow him into heaven. As we look for this, we must desire and ask now to hear our names from his lips in the way of constant admonition and exhortation; and as constantly, and with corresponding love, our hearts must say to him, "Master!"

"Master! may we ever say,
Taken from the world away,
See thy faithful servants, see,
Ever gazing up to thee.
Grant, though parted from our sight,
High above yon azure height,
Grant our souls may thither rise,
Following thee beyond the skies.

"Ever upward let us move,
Wafted on the wings of love,
Looking when our Lord shall come,
Looking for a happier home.
There we shall with thee remain,
Partners of thy endless reign,
There thy face unclouded see,
Find a heaven of heavens in thee."

IX.

THE WALK TO EMMAUS.

"And it came to pass, that while they communed together, and reasoned, Jesus himself drew near, and went with them."

Perhaps these two men lived at Emmaus, for when they arrived there, they invited the stranger, who had joined them on their way, to abide with them. Perhaps they had been to Jerusalem for to worship. "And they talked together of all these things which had happened." Never had a week, since creation, comprised such events, nor had creation witnessed events more interesting and important. These two men, not of the number of the twelve, were, however, Christian believers; the name of one of them, only, Cleopas, we know. "They communed together, and reasoned." The tomb of Christ has been opened, and the body is not there. What means this? Where is he? They asked questions of each other; the one expressed a doubt, the other a hope; he a difficulty, and the other a solution.

So they reasoned together in great darkness; and the blind was leading the blind.

A man drew near and passed along the same road. Their earnestness, their frequent exclamation, their lifting up of their hands, their deep-drawn sighs, warranted a kind inquiry, "What manner of communications are these that ye have one with another as ye walk and are sad?" There was only one subject, it seemed to them, which could then be thought of. "Art thou only a stranger in Jerusalem, and hast not known the things which are come to pass there in these days?"

We read that "counsel in the heart of man is like deep waters; but a man of understanding will draw it out." This stranger evidently knew how to lead on the conversation, and draw out the secret thoughts and feelings of the two men; nor did they need much urging, but told him of Jesus of Nazareth, 'and how the chief priests and our rulers delivered him to be condemned to death, and have crucified him. But we trusted that it had been he which should have redeemed Israel, and besides all this, to-day is the third day since these things were done,' that third day of which he repeatedly spoke. Whether he is risen or not, we cannot tell. The soldiers who watched him say, that some of our number came by night and stole him away while they slept. In confirmation of it, the priests and scribes say that one of his twelve disciples was certainly a thief, and that they are all, probably, thieves, and have stolen the body to persuade men that he is risen. Perhaps there is ground for this accusation; if Judas betrayed him for money, who knows that Philip has not deceived us, or that Matthew, or James, has not acted a foul part. Had Christ really risen from the dead, he would have appeared to his friends before this. He who came to them in a storm upon the lake, walking on the sea, knew full well what troubled hearts we must have had at his death, and how we looked for that 'third day,' which has come, and is nearly past; but where is he? Besides, had he risen from the dead, he would not have risen privately. Was the sun darkened when he was crucified? What signs and wonders might we not have expected when he came to life! Did the earth quake, the rocks rend, the dead rise, when he died? Surely his resurrection would have been hailed by all nature with demonstrations of joy, and not only the dead, but all heaven would have signified their more intense interest in such a triumph over the Saviour's enemies. Nor would he have failed to use his resurrection to confound his foes. We have borne ridicule and insults as the friends of our crucified master; he would have come forth from the tomb, if alive, in a manner that would have shaken Jerusalem to its foundations, and forever have silenced his foes. But he is gone from his tomb. Angels, indeed, say, or rather our women say, that he is risen. The women must have been deceived, and yet the body was not there.

But we trusted it had been he which should have redeemed Israel.

The stranger could hear no more. "O fools, and slow of heart to believe all that the prophets have spoken." We are willing to be called fools when a man has good news for us, and we care not if we are confounded and put to shame, may but our fears be proved to be without foundation. The inquiring stranger, this apparently uninformed man, this Parthian, or Cretan, this wayfaring man, though a fool in their first impressions of him, suddenly appeared possessed of perfect knowledge on the subject which perplexed and distressed them. He undertook to show that all which had happened was precisely in accordance with the Bible. He brought to mind such words as those from Zechariah; "Awake, O sword, against my shepherd, and against the man which is my fellow, saith the Lord of hosts; smite the shepherd, and the sheep shall be scattered;" and from Daniel: "And after threescore and two weeks shall Messiah be cut off, but not for himself;" and from Micah: "They shall smite the judge of Israel with a rod upon the cheek." He reminded them that Isaiah said: "He was taken from prison and from judgment, and who shall declare his generation? for he was cut off out of the land of the living; for the transgression of my people was he stricken. And he made his grave with the wicked and with the rich in his death." David foretold respecting his garments parted, and that for his vesture they would cast lots. He uttered the very words which the crucifiers used: "He trusted in the Lord that he would deliver him; let him deliver him, seeing he delighteth in him." Then beginning at Moses, no doubt he reminded them of the paschal lamb and scape-goat, and of the two birds, one of which was to be killed in sacrifice, and the other, dipped in his fellow's blood, was to go free. All this plainly foretold a suffering Messiah. But their conversation was interrupted by their arrival at Emmaus, and as the two men turned toward their house, the stranger, as any modest stranger would have done, kept on, or 'made as though he would have gone further.' In the beautiful spirit of eastern hospitality, "they constrained him, saying, Abide with us, for it is toward evening, and the day is far spent. And he went in to tarry with them."

And now their interest in the stranger grew to wonder and astonishment. Suddenly their guest became their host. "And it came to pass as he sat at meat with them, he took bread, and blessed it, and brake, and gave to them." What new surprise was there! A beneficiary has assumed to be benefactor; he repays their benefit with a benediction; it was their own bread which he was eating, yet he assumes to bless it, and break it, and offer it to them! No time ensued for inquiry, or for the expression of surprise. 'And their eyes were opened, and they knew him, and he vanished out of their sight.' Christ is risen. Risen? we have been walking with him; he has been talking with us, he has been a guest at our board. They asked one of the other if he ever had such feelings during a conversation, if discourse ever excited such peculiar emotions. "And they said one to another, Did not our heart burn within us while he talked with us by the way, and while he opened to us the Scriptures?"

Where did they sleep that night? Could they sleep at all? Could they sleep at Emmaus? "They rose up the same hour and returned to Jerusalem."

What a different walk they now had; what different men they were; what a new world they were in; all nature seemed to them to be praising God; "now glowed the firmament with living sapphires;" the mountains and the hills broke forth before them into singing, and all the trees of the field clapped their hands.

They went to carry good tidings, but when they arrived, "they found the eleven gathered together, and them that were with them, saying, The Lord is risen indeed, and hath appeared unto Simon." Those two witnesses confirmed their faith by relating what things were done in the way, and how he was known of them in the breaking of bread.

"And as they thus spake, Jesus himself stood in the midst of them and said, Peace be unto you." Emmaus did not detain him that night; he knew that the two friends had hastened back to their company, and that there would be a scene of deep interest, as they received and gave intelligence respecting him. So he fulfilled that promise: "I will not leave you comfortless, I will come unto you." There was great kindness in the salutation which he gave that company, for who were they? Men who could not watch with him one hour; all but two had forsaken him and fled, and of these two, one soon denied him, and they seem to have given no credit to his promises. Yet he comes and stands in the midst of them and says, "Peace be unto you." Let us leave them here, and, reviewing the walk to Emmaus, see the instruction which it affords.

What was the object of Christ in so remarkable an appearance to these two men?

It does not seem that the object was to convince the residue, for when these two arrived, they were themselves saluted by the eleven with the information that Christ had risen. Besides, as they spake, Jesus himself appeared and stood in the midst of them.

We may, therefore, conclude that the walk to Emmaus, and all which was connected with it, was an illustration of the Saviour's love for the individuals of his people. We cannot find any great or important object, as it would generally be viewed, to warrant such an interview on the part of Christ with those two men; and we must therefore ascribe it wholly to the Saviour's regard for each of his friends. Here were two of them greatly distressed on his account. Sincere inquirers after the truth, they were, nevertheless, confounded by the failure of Christ to manifest himself in a public resurrection. This seems to have troubled them. They looked that his resurrection should be as public as his crucifixion, his triumph as signal as his defeat, but the secret disappearance of his body from the tomb, confirmed the current story that some of his disciples had stolen his body, and that, really, he had not risen.

Now perhaps these two men, in leaving Jerusalem, were leaving Christ, and his cause, and his friends, for ever, persuaded that the whole mystery of Christ's life and death had proved, at last, a deception, and they were prepared to add these things to the list of delusions, some of which, with a mixture of good deeds, had only raised the hopes of men to disappoint them. And now they were irrecoverably in despair, unless some further light from heaven should break forth. But it came to pass as they communed together and reasoned, Jesus himself drew near and went with them. Is not this like him? Did he not say, I know my sheep? If one or two out of a flock wander, or are caught in a thicket, or sink in mire, a shepherd needs no great public event or influence to make him leave the flock and go after that which is lost until he find it. The great blessedness of those who have Christ for a shepherd is, as much as any thing, in this, that every one enjoys his undivided love and care. As a shepherd's whole mind and strength are concentrated on one sheep in trouble, our good Shepherd as readily expends thought and care upon each of us as though we were his only charge. It is related as a wonderful thing of Philip of Macedon, that he could call every private soldier in his army by name. It were but a partial consolation and comfort if we enjoyed the love of God and the presence of Christ only in common with others; but while he loves the gates of Zion more than all the dwellings of Jacob, and where two or three are gathered together, in his name, he is pledged to come, still he tells us, (and he says it after exalting our conceptions of him as 'the high and lofty One that inhabiteth eternity, whose name is Holy, that dwelleth in the high and holy place,') that to this man he will look, even to him who is poor and of a contrite spirit, and who trembles at his word.

Therefore in the sadness and sorrow of these two loving but stricken hearts, Jesus found reason and opportunity enough for a special manifestation of his loving-kindness. We may, therefore, each have Christ's presence with us whenever we need it. 'The Lord is my Shepherd,' as well as the shepherd of Israel.

> "My noonday walks he shall attend,
> And all my midnight hours defend."

His first appearances after his resurrection were to individuals. When you pray, he is within reach of your voice; when you are sick, he is by your bed; when you are in perplexity and darkness, he draws nigh; at his table, he sups with you.

But it is a good thing when two of his friends hold communion with regard to him, or any thing relating to his cause. Never are we deeply interested in private, personal matters, or in a society, or in any project, without taking counsel of some friend. It is well for one who is interested in religion to converse with one who is in like circumstances; and if they together should seek Christ, they might be specially sure of his presence. It would show an interest and earnestness which he would not fail to regard. When two members of a congregation come to a pastor and tell him that they have agreed to be companions in seeking Christ, or that they have helped each other in finding him, few things bring greater pleasure to that pastor's heart. When they together draw near to Christ, and invoke his love and care, he does not forget the spirit of his promise to any two who shall agree on earth as touching one thing.

It is pleasant when two brothers, or two sisters, make each other confidential friends with regard to their religious feelings. The distance between members of the same family with regard to religious conversation and communion, the common saying and feeling, I can talk with every one else more freely than with those of my own family, is owing very much to a consciousness of inconsistency in little things which is recognized at home, and to those little differences, or faults, or trespasses, which make the thought of communing together in spiritual things, repulsive. Strangers do not know these easily besetting sins. But if we, members of the same family, seek sweet counsel together, if brothers, if sisters, would accustom themselves to pray together, if during some heavy calamity which has fallen on the house, or under the influence of some great blessing, they should begin this practice, and while their hearts are under the subduing influence of sorrow or joy, they should together seek God, and become attached as Christians by such communion with each other and with Christ, these petty inconsistencies would be greatly prevented, family ties would feel the more powerful bond of a divine love, family religion would be greatly promoted, there would be Christian friendships in families, beautiful and strong, and that sad distance and alienation which too often exists between the children of a family and extends through life, would be exchanged for that unity which is described by inspiration as "good and pleasant." One great device of Satan is to make disunion and alienation; love and concord are to him hateful; but our Saviour associated, in the minds of his disciples, with the memorial of his love to them, an act of condescension and kindness, in washing their feet, which ought to be remembered and applied by us in all our relations to one another as often, at least, as we sit together at his table. Husbands and wives who love Christ, are most perfectly furnished with opportunities for this Christian fellowship. Without formality, without previous agreement, they converse on things most deeply interesting which pertain to Christ and religion, and their souls make them like the chariots of Amminadib. O what a loss it is when a husband and wife can have no communion together about these things. Claudius Buchanan, writing to his sister, said, "While your dear husband is spared to you, and you are spared to him, enjoy as much spiritual converse together as possible. For when the separation comes, you will reproach yourselves bitterly if you have not been tenderly communicative on this subject."

One way in which Christ teaches and assists us is, by making us tell him our troubles. This is forcibly illustrated by this walk to Emmaus. Whenever our hearts seem as though they would break, and we go alone, or with a friend, and spread our complaints before Christ, whenever the burden is so great that we fall down before God and rehearse all our grief, it is always the case, as in the instance now before us, that it is he who is making us relate our sorrows, and plead our cause, in order that we may have full views of the difficulty, and appreciate the help which he only can give, and be prepared to receive answers of peace. Thus he did with these two men. "What things?" he said. He assumes to be an inquirer, and draws from them the full measure of their trouble, and lets them see it clearly by stating it themselves, and dwelling upon it, to convince him how great it is; and then he proceeds to help them. Thus he delays to answer prayer for help, because we have not yet seen and felt the diversified nature of our affliction; it is made to turn its sharper points upon us, slowly and surely, till we feel ready to die, and then we can best feel our ill desert, and understand the depth of his mercy. So when we cast our burden upon him, he fulfils the promise that he will sustain not merely the "burden," but "thee." As a way-worn traveller on foot asks one who drives by, to carry his burden, and the kind man says, I will take you also, by casting his burden on this man, the man sustained him. The burden may not be parted from us; but grace is given sufficient for the burden and the thorn. When we are sick, for example, with some perplexing illness, how seldom do men consult God, and lay their case in his hands before consulting a physician. Here was Asa's sin, when he was diseased in his feet. But when we consult God, his chosen method is to make us consult men. He might have relieved the mind of the praying Cornelius by direct disclosures; but no, he must send for Peter; and Saul of Tarsus could easily have had visions and revelations of the Lord, but instead of this, Ananias must go and lay his hands upon him.

In connection with this, it is also interesting to notice, in this walk to Emmaus, how Christ honors the

Old Testament. Instead of beginning with his own life, he began at Moses and all the prophets. One instructive way for an intelligent, thinking inquirer who would fully know the doctrine of Christ, is to begin at Moses; and therefore the epistle to the Hebrews, which is well suited to that class of minds, is, very much of it, a commentary on Moses and Aaron as types of Christ. If the Old Testament was enough, in the Saviour's judgment, to inform and satisfy those men about him, what can we, with the finished revelation of God in our hands, need more? But what is worse than to destroy the confidence of a man in this Bible! As we meet with sly insinuations against it in our popular literature, it is pleasant to contrast with them the simplicity and artlessness with which these sacred penmen tell us, so honestly, of their doubts about Christ's resurrection, the event on which every thing relating to Christianity turned. But it seems to have been a hard thing to convince them. They were slow of heart to believe; Christ needed to make them handle him; and he eat before them; and even then, all were not persuaded; and at the very close, on the mount of ascension, it is said that they believed, "but some doubted." How cruel to charge these simple-hearted men with stealing, and palming a lie on the world; and yet is it less cruel to represent them as inventing a story in any degree, or narrating any thing which was not true to the utmost letter?

The darkest methods of God's providence are frequently his choicest blessings. The way to deliver Israel was, to pour darkness and seeming confusion upon the hopes of believers by the selfsame events which, in all their sadness and gloom, the prophets had testified must happen. If any great calamity is happening to you, and you love God, you may be sure that it will be attended or followed by some great good. "Ascribe ye strength unto God; his excellency is over Israel, *and his strength is in the clouds.*"

We ought to believe. The evidence in religion is overwhelming. Pitiably weak and foolish, as well as inconsistent, is our inability to believe the most important things, under the most powerful evidence, yet believing fables and follies on the slightest foundation. We should come with our difficulties to God, in prayer, and remember the truth of Luther's inscription in his study: "To have prayed well is to have studied well." God the Spirit can do for us, in a Sabbath day's journey, more than all books and teachers and the studies of a lifetime without him, can accomplish. We should ask for faith as we ask for health, or escape from drowning, or help in a dying hour.

Unless we make the sufferings of Christ the first object of his coming, we have no such Redeemer as the Bible represents. "Ought not Christ to have suffered these things, and to enter into his glory?" The prophets were "searching diligently what, and what manner of time, the Spirit of Christ which was in them did signify, when it testified beforehand the sufferings of Christ and the glory that should follow." The great defect in the opinions of many respecting Christ is, His sufferings are not, in their view, his main object. They confirm his example; they happened in the way of martyrdom; and they powerfully attest his sincerity, and his doctrines. Such is not the Messiah of the Old Testament and the Jesus of the New. Some make the declared object of his sufferings and of his blood only metaphorical. They have no Redeemer. Christ was "slain from the foundation of the world," his sufferings and death having an effect as soon as man fell. If we would "behold his glory," as he prayed that we may, we must see it through his sufferings, for he suffered these things that he might "enter into his glory."

As there was no reason why these early disciples should love Christ and be interested in him, and his cause, more than we, like them we should have our Christian friendships, growing out of attachment to him and his service. Christian friendships attract the notice, they secure the company, of Christ. We must love and prize our church-meetings, endeavor to make them more and more spiritual and Christlike, removing from them every thing which interrupts harmony, and conducting them so as to look confidently for the Saviour's presence in them. We must cultivate habits of social prayer, join with one another in visits to the throne of grace; the walk to Emmaus, and from Emmaus, may be enjoyed often with some Christian friend, our eyes opened and our heart burning within us, and a Saviour believed in and adored, at our side. We shall have such converse in the heavenly Jerusalem; those who love each other here, in Christ, will love each other there; brothers, sisters, you will not be afraid, nor ashamed, to manifest Christian feelings to each other there. The love of pious husbands and wives here, will be surpassed there, for they will love each other, chiefly, as they see the likeness of Christ in each other, and together behold him walking with them.

When those men went to Emmaus with Christ at their side, other travellers, no doubt, passed by, and noticed three men walking and talking together; but they knew not that little group of three, nor what eternal interest was in the subject of their conversation. They knew not the Lamb of God, they knew not the final Judge of men and angels, in communion with these two Christians. Our table to-day, like the table of Emmaus, has one with whom you would esteem it an honor to sit, did you know him. He is the risen Redeemer, our ascended Lord, our Intercessor; he will be our Judge. When your friends come home from the table, they will be able to tell what things were done in the way, and how he was made known to them in the breaking of bread. O that you would anticipate them, when you meet them again, and say, 'The Lord is risen indeed, and hath appeared unto me.' With you in your retirement, while his people are at his table, he who drew near to those two men in their lonely and sad walk, will love to be; and he will break the bread of life to you alone, and bless you, as he blessed those two at their table, at Emmaus.

And now, Saviour, we have, as it were, reached Emmaus. We have spread a table for thee, and what a table! We wait for thee to take the bread, and bless it, and give it to us, for it is thy body; and here is thy blood! Our eyes are opened; we know thee; thou wilt not vanish from our sight. With some of us, "the day is far spent;" and with some who little suspect it. "Abide with us;" go with us from thy table, to our table at home, to our duties, to our enjoyments, to our trials. Through life, in death, "abide with us," till we also rise up, and return to JERUSALEM, and find the eleven gathered together and them that are with them!

X.

THOU PREPAREST A TABLE BEFORE ME.

"THOU PREPAREST A TABLE BEFORE ME IN THE PRESENCE OF MINE ENEMIES."

WHEN we examine and interpret this expression, we almost shrink from the singular confidence which represents the Most High in such an act of condescension. But the difficulty is only with our faith; for, when we compare these words with the representations, in the New Testament, of the love of God to men, and notice the figures and symbols there employed, as well as the terms of filial confidence and love in the Old Testament, we find that David used only a warrantable degree of assurance in saying, "Thou preparest a table before me." It is a metaphor, which implies great things,— God preparing for a man a table.

Among the pleasures of life, a table suitably provided and well arranged, is a soul-reviving sight. They are wise who study a proper degree of pleasure, as well as ordinary comforts, in spreading their board, and the family is favored which has a tasteful hand, ingenious in giving pleasure, to make their table inviting by those nameless arts which love and care, independently of wealth, supply. A well-prepared table is not merely a place to appease hunger. The eye is pleased with its order and fitness; the impression is made that there has been design and judgment exercised there, by which means there are moral influences exerted upon us, of no small importance. He who has his spirits cheered, and pleasurable impressions made upon him, once, twice, or three times a day, by a neat, well disposed, though humble, board, if he be not a churl, will be far more useful, as well as happier, in all the relations of life, than one to whom his table suggests no such thoughts and feelings. The wife whose mind and heart are both employed in this thing, need not feel that she lives to no purpose. It is not the satisfying of hunger, merely, but the moral influences connected with doing it, which she promotes; and doing it well, she binds her family together with sweet influences which children feel and remember in far distant years, and in other homes. What a joy it is to a careworn man to be invited by one whom he loves, to a repast, though it be only a dinner of herbs, which thoughtfulness of his comfort has provided for him. And when at times something is done to surprise him, or with his friends, he sits at the board where that same taste and skill which spread the feast, presides, and sheds happiness upon the circle, he does not deserve to be blest if he be not grateful in no ordinary measure.

That which the best and dearest earthly friend does for a man, day by day, God is represented as doing for one who loves him and trusts in him. What must a table be which God has spread for us!

A regard for our common wants is implied in so doing. There are things done for us by those who love us, at home, which wealth has no power to buy, ministrations of kindness dictated by no mercenary feelings, and having regard to that ordinary comfort and happiness which are of more importance than great services. My God, who knows my downsitting and uprising, and numbers the hairs of my head, does not confine his goodness to extraordinary acts, but he bestows things on which happiness depends more than upon unusual favors. "Thou preparest a table before me." God condescends to my ordinary need; nothing is beneath him which is an object of my need.

But there is frequently a special preparation even of ordinary blessings, by the hand of God. Not merely our daily bread, but things are provided for us in want or distress, things in themselves cheap and common, but provided under circumstances which make them seem like a table in the wilderness. Will God do this? Our experience is full of it. Yet it is a wonderful representation to make, — the Most High preparing a table for a needy man. "Which of you having a servant ploughing or feeding cattle will say unto him by and by when he is come from the field, Go and sit down to meat?" But God prepares a table for his servant; it is that which the man's own servants would be expected to do, or that which his dearest friend would love to do for him. They who spend much time and thought in solving mysteries which never can be explained, would do well to leave them and study God's unsearchable love. There is more in this to exercise their faith, to excite wonder, to reward contemplation, to improve the mind and heart, than can be found in large volumes upon certain controverted subjects.

It is in the way of triumph over enemies, that God is pleased sometimes to prepare for a man who loves and serves him, some special and noticeable blessing. Much is said in the Bible about injurious treatment from our fellow men; prayer is very frequently rendered with reference to this, and deliverance from it is gratefully acknowledged. "Let not the foot of pride come against me, and let not the hand of the wicked remove me." There is a power to injure us which is not dignified enough to be reckoned with principalities, yet it has great ability for mischief and discomfort, and that is, "the power of the dog." To be run at, and to be followed, by currish spirits, base, unreasonable natures, is an annoyance from which it is often most difficult to escape; to resist, provokes it; to flee, emboldens it, and we pray for some power to call it off from us. "Deliver my soul from the lion, my darling from the power of the dog." David prays to be delivered from a certain trouble, "lest they that hate me rejoice when I am moved." When Hannah was made happy, she could not help thinking and speaking about "the adversaries," and rejoicing in God over them. So it was with the virgin Mary. It was natural for her to think of those who had been proud toward her, and it was gratifying to think of being exalted above her state in life, over those who had looked down upon her. There was no sinful pride in these feelings, for there was nothing malign or vindictive in them. As we read her beautiful song, we are made to say, Surely, God has prepared a table for Mary in the presence of her enemies. This is an envious world. Solomon said, that "for every right work, a man is envied of his neighbor." James asks us, "know ye not that the spirit which dwelleth in us lusteth to envy?"—that it is our natural disposition to be moved at the prosperity and happiness of others? Blessed state, when "each the bliss of all shall view, with infinite delight," and be as truly happy in the happiness of others as in his own;—in which case there will indeed be fulness of joy and pleasures forevermore.

When God appears with some token of favor toward one who has had enemies, or there have been those who have oppressed or slighted him, a good man has two sets of feelings. He has a feeling of love and tenderness toward his enemies. With no pride of superiority, he is made superior to them by the hand of God, and the effect is to make him kind and forgiving. Another feeling is, extreme gratification in seeming to be vindicated. His natural sense of justice is gratified. There is much exulting language in the histories of holy men on this subject. "For thou, Lord, hast lifted me up, and hast not made mine enemies to triumph over me." One of the blessings promised to him that "considereth the poor," is, "and thou wilt not deliver him into the will of his enemies." Our natural love of justice, our hatred of wrong and oppression, are encouraged when it is said, for example, "When a man's ways please the Lord, he maketh even his enemies to be at peace with him." Or, "When mine enemies came upon me to eat up my flesh, they stumbled and fell." How many ways God has of blessing us. When he undertakes to do a man good, how precious are his thoughts toward him, how great is the sum of them. When he giveth quietness, who then can make trouble?

All these things, rich and great as they are, nevertheless are of inferior value and import, and are brought to view only that we may better appreciate something which far surpasses them. When we read to-day, "Thou preparest a table before me," think of the preparations made and now awaiting us, for the Lord's Supper.

God has prepared this table. Eminently true is this, and most affectingly true. Who but God could have prepared this table? All heaven could not have spread and furnished it. There was no eye to pity, no arm to save. Then it was said, "Deliver him from going down to the pit; I have found a ransom." We may say with confidence that to angels this table is the greatest wonder in the world. It was the most difficult thing to furnish. It is the most interesting object. Bethlehem, Gethsemane, Calvary, the manger, garden, cross, concentrate all their rays of light and love here. If angels were to preach, they would love to stand here. They come to see this sight, they commune together about it; they desire to look into it; always new to us, it never grows old with them. If angels could not have furnished this table, kings, princes, nobles of the earth never could have done it. The wealth of Crœsus and Midas would have been only the small dust in the balance, toward it. Cleopatra may dissolve pearls to drink them, but no mention should be made of coral nor of pearls here; for the price of it is above rubies.

And when we say that God 'prepared' this table, we are led to think of that stupendous plan which was connected with it, far back in the councils of eternity, and of that great dispensation of atoning rites which for four thousand years held the world in a state of expectation, and in pupilage, to be instructed into its meaning. This table was provided by a sacrifice which exhausted the treasury of heaven. God manifest in the flesh spread it, in person, with his own hands. His humiliation, sufferings, and death are here. As our words are diminished and suppressed in proportion as our feelings are intense, so the infinite meaning of this table has chased away all form and ceremony from it beyond a bare outline of an ordinance, just sufficient to make it cognizable by the senses. What severe and awful simplicity is here! These two symbols only, simple and plain, dependent on no forms for their efficacy, nor on the vessels which hold them, whether of gold, or silver, or wood, or earth, are the Lord's Supper. Their single signification is, the Lord's death: an object remaining the same from the beginning, 'until he come;' thus beautifully holding us in communion with all the people of God in times past and at present, amid changes of all other customs, and variety and contrariety of opinion, and strange languages, and also setting our faces toward that great event, his final coming. "Ye do show the Lord's death until he come," Judge of the living and of the dead, in the glory of his father and of his holy angels; and such is he who spread, who furnished this table and calls to every human being, "This do, in remembrance of me."

And now, in recollection of what has been said respecting a table, as to the place it holds among the influences of our daily life, it is pleasant to think that this great commemorative and admonitory appointment is associated with a table. A table is an emblem of home. Influences centre round our tables not exceeded in their power and interest elsewhere. Happy hours pass by, bonds of love are formed, are nurtured, communion has its secret places, friendships are cemented and alienations are healed, there. We read of a treacherous enemy who, on being detected, was not put to death because he had eaten with the man whom he had injured, at the man's own board. What joyful meetings and gatherings does a table witness; and there we specially see the bounties of God's providence. The custom is founded in nature, of acknowledging God by prayer, at our tables; asking a blessing is a poor idea of that service; it is the recognition by a dependent creature of the hand that feeds him. The table is the central point of all domestic comfort and blessings. Christ speaks of heaven under the similitude of a table; "ye shall eat and drink at my table in my kingdom."

When Christianity chooses a table as the symbol of her choicest gifts, we see how eminently social and benevolent its nature is; communion, fellowship, giving, the rites of hospitality, kindred, home, invitation, refreshment, invigoration, and cheer, and every pleasurable idea which comes at the thought of a welcome table, are implied in it.

But we must carry the idea still further. "Before me," each of us can say, and he must, in truth say, —

"thou preparest a table — before me." No human being in the wilds of heathenism could be found and brought in, through the grace of God, to this supper, who could not in the fullest sense, equally with each fellow-creature, say this. "Before me," a rebel, to win, and reconcile me; a lost soul, to redeem and save me; a starving soul, to feed me with the bread which came down from heaven. But they who actually partake of it say, "before me," in a peculiar sense. Instead of being left to a wretched choice, as they are who had rather starve than come, I am here, and "thou preparest a table before me." Thou makest me to sit down, and girdest thyself, and comest forth to serve me. There are gifts and blessings which come upon us sometimes, whose only effect, for a season, is amazement. Such is this, to be led by a hand that "sweetly forced us in," overcoming all our difficulties, repugnance, and every thing which keeps others away, and making us kings and priests to God, sitting together in heavenly places in Christ Jesus, belonging to the church of all ages, past, present, and to come, in heaven and in earth; and while others say, "How can this man give us his flesh to eat," making us eat his body and drink his blood, as an expression to us that his love spared nothing for our sake, and that he seeks to incorporate and identify us each with himself, members of his body, of his flesh, and of his bones. We cannot contend with thee in thy love, any more than with thine omnipotence. We are like those little pools upon the sea-shore at low tide; and now the ocean floods us, and we are lost in it.

"Nay, but I yield! I yield!
I can hold out no more;
I sink by dying love compelled,
And own thee conqueror!

"Come, and possess me whole,
Nor hence again remove;
Settle and fix my wavering soul
With all thy weight of love."

There are spectators of our communion season who are out of our sight. One, is the arch enemy of God and man; and if we believe in the existence and agency of evil spirits, that great apostate angel and his confederates look on when the Lord's Supper is administered to us. "Thou preparest a table before me in the presence of mine enemies." As nothing in this world represents to the view of holy angels such sublime, affecting interests as the Lord's Supper, so there is nothing which to Satan and his angels is such a memorial of their woe. Man was Satan's victim in this newly created world; a race of creatures had, by his instigation, apostatized, and would have peopled the realms of darkness with rebels in league with fallen angels against God, or would have become the subjects of infernal malignity, gratifying a diabolical love of misery by the torments which their despots would have inflicted. The plan was successful in its beginning; man, the sinner, without the shadow of a reason, broke his allegiance to God, and straightway incurred the doom which had already fallen on those who had sinned in heaven. Sovereign mercy interposed, providing a way of pardon for man, and left the tempter and his angels under the everlasting curse. Then followed the astonishing work of human redemption, of which this sacramental rite is the memorial. The sight of a company of human beings around this table must be, of all sights on earth, a mournful, a distressing spectacle to these our enemies.

It reminds them of their own irrecoverable ruin. Our restoration shows them the possibility which there was, in the nature of things, that they could have been redeemed. Perhaps they thought, when they sinned, and afterward, that God could not forgive sin; their own jurisprudence suggested no expedient by which it could be done; and their experience in the legislation of heaven furnished no precedent of the kind. When, therefore, they saw that God could be just and justify a sinner, that it was actually done, and done by the incarnation of Him who made them (for by him were all things created that are in heaven and that are in earth, visible and invisible, whether they be thrones, or dominions, or principalities, or powers,) and that this God manifest in the flesh, passed by them, and bestowed on the sinner, man, their victim, this unspeakable gift, we may suppose that their wrath knew no bounds. So that as often as they see the Lord's table spread, it is a hateful sight; they hate the sight of the Bible, of a true minister of Jesus, of a real Christian, of a good book, and of many other things; but the sight of the Lord's Supper and forgiven sinners partaking of it, aggravates their misery. When heaven rejoices over the reception of a goodly number, or even of one soul, into the church on earth, it is a signal for new distress among those disappointed and miserable beings who are again notified by every act of salvation, that their judgment lingereth not, and their damnation slumbereth not.

All which they can do, therefore, is, to hinder, as far as possible, the good effect of this great ordinance upon us. Glad are they when by the suggestion of doubts and fears, they can prevent a troubled soul from deriving benefit from this scene of love and mercy. Some they would persuade that they were precipitate, and then they haunt and worry them with their upbraidings. Upon all of us they practise temptations, so that by the commission of sin, or the neglect of duty, or want of suitable preparation, the ordinance may fail of its designed effect. Are they not busy with their fiery darts, during the participation of the supper? Whatever may distract the mind of a communicant, whether it be by untimely or unprofitable remarks of the minister, or by evil associations in the thoughts of the Christian, by animosity, or by prejudice, by the sight of one who has been, or still is, an enemy, in all manner of ways the emissaries of darkness are, no doubt, busy with us, when God has prepared this table for us in their presence. They can injure him only through us. And then, to borrow the blessed Leighton's figure of the arch pirate, who lies in wait for the richest ships, these foes of ours are watching for us as we go away from the supper. For if, as the Saviour says, when the seed of the word is cast into the hearts by the preacher, " then cometh the wicked one and catcheth away that which was sown," surely they must find it greatly to their advantage if they can prevent us from retaining, for any length of time, and especially from reducing to practice, the instructions afforded by the ordinance of the supper.

Therefore, if we remember that God has prepared the table before us in the presence of these enemies, we shall do well if we go to it, and partake of it, and come away from it, as in their presence.

We should examine ourselves to see if we do repent and forsake sin, which has been the occasion of such disaster; which cost angels their thrones, and binds them in chains under darkness; so that to save us from the same just condemnation with them, the amazing sacrifice for sin was made. As we walk to the house of God on the communion Sabbath, as we take our seats in view of the table, and as we receive the memorials of the Saviour's body and blood, the thought that we are made a spectacle unto angels, with such probable feelings on their part with regard to the supper, and toward us, will naturally make us feel how great a thing it is to engage in that transaction. It will excite our gratitude for the distinguishing goodness of God toward man, and for that redemption which we see in the case of fallen angels could as justly have been withheld from us as from them. The Lord's Supper being the divinely appointed representation of that great work which distinguishes the moral government of God, to have a place at that table is, in the esteem of lost angels, to occupy a seat higher than any earthly throne; it is a place which they regard as second only to a throne in glory, and indeed as the step to that throne.

What must they think of those who, having been communicants, and holding still a right to sit at the table, yet because they are strangers where they now reside, go away from the table, though included in the invitation to commune? No light thing would keep them away, could they obtain a reversal of their doom, or a temporary reprieve, for a new probation.

Do they not look with eager interest over the company of communicants, thinking whether any from that assembly may finally be made their prey? They know that the promise is only to those who endure unto the end, and therefore they ply their terrible arts for our destruction.

But with all that is oppressively solemn in our responsibilities, and fitted to make us fear, let us not be dismayed. He who spread that table, came to destroy him that had the power of death, that is the devil. The roaring lion is chained, and his chain is in the hand of Christ. He could lead him into our assembly to-day, a trembling captive, and make him cry, Art thou come to torment me before the time? All the power of the enemy cannot hurt us; devils and wicked men, together, cannot hurt us; we can hurt ourselves, by neglect and sin, but not because Satan and all his hosts are able to tempt us above that which we are able to bear. Safe and happy under the protection of our infinite Saviour and friend, let us go to each successive communion season with more intelligent views of truth, with a higher standard of duty, with deeper impressions of what it is to be saved, and to be lost, remembering that at the last day we shall either "judge angels," or be condemned in their presence to the punishment from which we had been redeemed, but from which they had no Redeemer.

"In the presence of mine enemies." Imagine all the enemies whom you have ever been compelled to regard as such, gathered together at the door of the place of worship, or seated in some conspicuous part of the house, and in sight of you. On you alone they fix their eyes, as you receive the emblems of the Saviour's body and blood.

Now, is there one among them toward whom you exercise an unforgiving spirit? He has injured you greatly; perhaps you have a deep and a just sense of the wrong which he has committed, and you are wholly in the right. At all events, what are your feelings toward him? what has been your conduct with regard to his trespass? Have you ever left your gift before the altar, to go and be reconciled? and have you now returned, from a well meant, though unsuccessful endeavor, to be at peace with him? You may then ask for mercy in view of the ten thousand talents which you owe to the justice, to the grace of God, you having forgiven that enemy his trespasses. Is he, in your apprehension, an unconverted man? This is enough to subdue every unkind feeling toward him, as you sit at the table of Christ. Is he a professor of religion? a member of the same church with yourself? There are differences of opinion and practice among good men which sometimes separate them from one another, but the table of Christ should witness sincere protestations of good-will and desires for peace, on the part of every one who receives the sacrament of the supper.

Let us permit those enemies to bring each his complaint to our conscience. Whom have I injured? Whom have I defrauded? Whom have I treated in an unbecoming manner? As they look upon me at the table of Christ, can they justly accuse me before him, who knows my heart, of any wilful injury or neglect? "Thou preparest a table before me in the presence of mine enemies." At such a table, let me resolve that if I have an enemy, I will have no enmity, toward him or any human being, as God for Christ's sake has forgiven me.

It is a peculiarity of the table of Christ that it can receive and entertain an indefinite number. Always has it been said, and to-day it is proclaimed again, "And yet there is room." See the vacant seats around you, and before you. See how many go away. If the communion season has its proper effect upon us, we shall each go away purposing to do something toward bringing others to the possession of these infinite blessings.

There is another table of which the Saviour speaks, when he promises some that they should eat and drink at his table, in his kingdom. When we think how many come to the table on earth, we are reminded of the great multitude which will come from the four winds to sit with Christ above. And will each one who reads these lines, be there? You are invited; but perhaps you are one who has not yet accepted the invitation.

Supposing this to be the communion Sabbath, what

if you should purpose with yourself that, by the help of God, when the next communion Sabbath arrives, you will be in such circumstances that, if it were in accordance with the proper regulations of the church, you would be able to join in commemoration of the Saviour's death, at his table. We will suppose that the interval between the communion seasons is a month. During the present month, you are to strive to enter in at the strait gate. If there be mercy in heaven for you, if there is grace there sufficient for you, if the advice and help of others can avail any thing, if the kingdom of heaven yet suffers violence and the violent take it by force, you are this month to secure the salvation of your soul.

What if you had come from eternity, with a month allowed you to repent of your sins, and accept pardon through Christ? Bend your whole soul to the effort, as in such a case you would not fail to do; seek advice, be directed; and having seen, as you will not fail to see, what you must do to be saved, remember that the time is short, and that whatsoever your hand findeth to do, you must do it with your might. When that next communion Sabbath arrives, many, very many, will be beyond the reach of all such opportunities. To-day they will go from the sight of the Lord's table, little thinking that the next time it appears before them, it will be in their remembrances of earth, beyond the limits of hope.

This table is spread again and again; you may go away, and return, and find it spread, and the access to it as free as infinite love and the outstretched hands of Christ can make it. But, there is a time when they that are ready will go in with him to the marriage, and the door will be shut. May you obtain the wedding garment before it is too late, and so be a guest forever at the table of Christ, in his kingdom!

XI.

THE SACRAMENTAL HYMN.

"AND WHEN THEY HAD SUNG A HYMN, THEY WENT OUT INTO THE MOUNT OF OLIVES."

IT is commonly said that there is no such singing heard elsewhere as at the Lord's table. It is certainly true that we are never in so good a frame of mind to enjoy it, as at the sacramental season. It may also be true that the mysterious connection between the feelings and the voice, accounts for some of the peculiar excellence in melody at such times. Dying persons while singing have, not unfrequently, been known to utter strains of music not only unusual even for them as singers, but of strange beauty, wild and free, yet within the laws of harmony, with inimitable transitions, like the glide on the strings of the guitar and violin, and with the plaintiveness of the untutored wind among the strings of the Æolian harp. If we ever reach a point at which grace for a time holds nature in full control, and the spirit has the mastery over the flesh, and the passions, instead of being quenched, are like the living creatures in the wheels of Ezekiel's vision, it is when we have been contemplating Christ crucified, and sorrow, forgiveness, love, hope, and new-born purposes have made our hearts like creation with its vigorous conceptions when the Spirit of God had brooded over it, so that the first opportunity to utter our feelings in a song, is as when it was said, Let there be light. Our sacred passions then find expression and manifestation; those who are skilled in music pour forth strains with a vigor that controls the inharmonious notes which, in less energetic singing, have such fatal power over the current of sound. Probably it is not mere fancy which gives rise to the common feeling with regard to the singing at the communion season.

Singing concluded the celebration of the Passover Supper, so that this first sacramental hymn was, in a sense, the song of Moses and of the Lamb. The passover was a constant memorial of national, domestic, individual salvation in a time of deep distress and peril; a song of praise well became that celebration. There was, as it were, a transmigration of soul from the Passover to the Lord's Supper; a change of a chrysalis into a higher order of life. The Lord's Supper was not instituted at the Feast of Tabernacles; nor was the day of atonement converted into the Christian sacrament; but the Passover was the point of transition from ritual thanksgivings, under the law, to the perpetual memorial of our deliverance from bondage. The pious Jews sang the passover hymn under the mingled feelings of a jubilee, and of a solemn religious rite; but when they came to see Christ as their passover, when Aaron gave place in their hearts to Jesus, (to effect which was a great object of the epistle to the Hebrews,) and when the paschal lamb became, in their view, a mere type and shadow of the Lamb of God, we can conceive that the place was shaken where they were assembled together, under the influence of their spring-tide love to their Redeemer. Far more expressive, however, should be our sacramental hymns, with the whole history of the gospel in our hands. And if, with such prospects as the coming history of redemption opens to our view, we did not sing at the Lord's Supper as we sing nowhere else, it would seem that the stones would cry out.

Some, indeed, may sing acceptably to the ear of Christ who never raise a note with their voice, but still the public singing of those who love him, is better to him than secret love, for the same reasons that he "loveth the gates of Zion more than all the dwellings of Jacob." Therefore they who can sing, with the understanding and with the spirit together, do best fulfil this part of the sacramental service, and render more acceptable honor to the master of the feast.

Their voices, each of them, though blended with the great volume of sound, are discerned by his ear, more perfectly than we can trace, in a large choir, the captivating 'alto,' which fixes attention by its imitative nature as it follows the 'air,' like the second rainbow around the meteor itself; and whether the voice be of a child, at the Supper, early tuned to sacred praise, or the noble voice of the man in his prime, or the melody of her whose soul, in its love to Christ, is itself a melody, Jesus hears it, follows it through, accepts the offering, and loves the giver.

The members of choirs would seem to have a spiritually presumptive right to places at the Lord's table, or rather, the table has a peculiar claim to them. Every member of a choir in a Christian congregation ought to be there. What strains there would be at our communion seasons if the chief singers were all there. If the son of Jesse dedicated many of his Psalms "to the chief singer on my stringed instruments," the Son of David surely has a right to dedicate the Sacramental Hymns to the chief singers of his sanctuaries, and to require their presence there. After enjoying the musical gifts of our friends during the day, we are sorry to miss them at the very time when our enjoyment of their help would be the greatest, and when they could do most, by offering praise, to glorify Christ. When the members of our choirs, one and all, take those places at the Lord's table which are waiting for them, ('and yet there is room') we may say as one of our hymns says of Christ's appearing 'in yonder cloud,' and of our gathering together unto him,

> "Then shall we sing more sweet, more loud,
> And Christ shall be our song."

"And when they had sung a hymn." — Then, perhaps, Jesus sang. Did he indeed sing? Jesus wept, and though we do not read of many common expressions of pleasure by him, yet, he sang. We have no tradition, there is no record, with regard to his voice, though we read that "never man spake like this man;" "and all wondered at the gracious words which proceeded out of his mouth." If he sang, all was natural and expressive; he sang as he loved, and prayed, and went about doing good, with all his heart and soul, and under the influence of supreme love to his father. Deeply impressive must have been those articulations of sound from his lips, the sentiment uttered receiving force from his expression. Jesus sang, and in doing it, is not ashamed to call us brethren, saying, "I will declare thy name unto my brethren; in the midst of the church will I sing praise unto thee," which he did literally, when, with his little church of Apostles, he sung a hymn. There is nothing which interests us, in which, on inquiry, we cannot find that the Saviour was in some way, interested. He listens to those who sing his praise in every place; he understands music; he is the

Creator of music. He loves it, when it fulfils its noblest purpose, — to glorify him.

Perhaps in no way do those who sing engage his love more than when, each of them, in their retirement, they take a hymn of praise to Christ, and fixing their thoughts upon him, sing it before him, as an act of worship. No wonder if they find it difficult to get through with it, their emotions interrupting their utterance, and tears obscuring their sight, till they are

> "Rapt into sweet communion which transcends
> The imperfect utterance of prayer and praise."

No nearer approach than this is ever made to the enjoyments and employments of the heavenly world. Then let our songs abound; in private, let us often do, as Pliny tells the emperor Trajan the early Christians did in their assemblies, — 'sing a hymn to Christ as God;' and if at all times, when we sing together, we could thus sing with melody in our hearts unto the Lord, giving life and power to taste and skill, our common acts of praise would have much of the quality of the Sacramental Hymns.

We need more of the cheering, soothing influence of sacred music; the heart of man is bowed down with many a secret grief, oppressed with many cares, discouraged and ready to faint with weakness and sin. O for great companies of pious hearts in all our congregations, with skilful voices, to bring in heaven, like spring, upon the winter of our life. Those churches which, by their organization, have religious societies connected with them, should have that precedency in directing this part of worship which they so properly, and by consent, have, with respect to the call and settlement of a minister; always, however, as in the latter case they are sure to do, if they act discreetly, regarding the general feelings and wishes. The highest degree of cultivation ought to be secured, musical talent should be brought into the service of sacred praise, and withal, though it is but the expression of an individual opinion, it seems probable that a well-trained choir is essential to cultivate the spirit of sacred music in a congregation, and that our Sacramental hymns will be sung in the most desirable manner in churches where there are well-trained choirs upon the Sabbath. In vain, therefore, do we argue from the singing at the Sacramental seasons, with which we all profess to be satisfied, that we can dispense with choirs. At the same time, the influence of a good choir which has a leader who makes this a chief object, may be, and, in foreign churches more perhaps than with us, it has the effect, to promote the exercise of sacred praise so generally that the congregation becomes like a well-trained choir.

If we wished to make our places of worship attractive to people at large by the singing, we should make it in the first place, scientifically correct, for the blind and the lame we do not offer to our governor; and being correct and in itself good, let it be seen that God is adored, that his fear and his love govern the service, and the effect will follow which the Apostle speaks of as inevitable in well-conducted religious services, — the secrets of a man's heart will be made manifest to him, "and so falling down on his face, he will worship God, and report that God is in you of a truth." Godliness in the conduct of this part of worship will be found to be profitable for all things, advancing the secular interests of the congregation, which we desire, of course, only for its effect in promoting the edification or salvation of men. But when the singing is a mere performance, we feel it at once as we immediately feel and detest affectation in prayer. When a piece is sung, and no one hears its words, whether they be Italian, Latin, or English, when the snatches of the operas or secular pieces bring in foreign associations, or when in the midst of a fervent, devotional strain of thought and feeling in a hymn, an unmeaning interlude, or a fanciful excursion on the organ obtrudes itself, formalism usurps the place of worship, and to what purpose is the multitude of such oblations but to draw upon us the displeasure of God? That God must be displeased, in many cases, with what is called our "good music" in his house, and with all the secular motives and feelings and language connected with it, that he sees in it nothing but a sacrifice to ourselves, and that he says of such sacrifices, "I will not smell in your solemn assemblies," no one can doubt who remembers that God is a spirit, and they that worship him must worship him in spirit and in truth. How far it has the effect to keep away the influences of the Holy Spirit, not only by its insidious displacement of truly spiritual feelings in all concerned, but by directly grieving him, is a question which deserves to be pondered by every church of Christ. The Holy Spirit must not be expected to favor that place of worship with his presence when the praises of God have no higher motive and end than to furnish what is called "good music." Good it ought to be; never should it be better than in the house of God, but as the oratory of a theatrical actor who should become a sincere preacher of Jesus, would cease to be theatrical yet be no less powerful, so music, instrumental, as well as vocal, in the house of God, must pass through minds, if not regenerated, imbued, at least, with religious sentiment, so as necessarily to awaken nothing in the mind of the worshipper but religious feelings, and surely not to interfere with such feelings.

These thoughts are offered in connection with the peculiarly sacred and solemn ordinance of the Lord's Supper, because few things do more, either to promote the presence and blessing of Christ and the Holy Spirit, or to grieve them, and few things contribute more to the comfort and strength of Christians, or to hinder the good influences of the sanctuary, than the service of song. We ought to pray more for divine instruction and blessing in this respect, for reasons not unlike those for which we invoke the divine blessing upon preachers and their efforts. Christ has consecrated the power of song by associating it with that ordinance of which he says, This do in remembrance of me. Let it be observed, in passing from this topic, that they who have the power to insinuate cheering or soothing sentiments or feelings by the power of the voice, do great good in a congregation by dispelling many a brooding thought which might otherwise become fixed melancholy; and to inspirit many a pilgrim in his way to God.

And as it is supposed to be the Communion Sabbath when these lines are read, it will be appropriate to say, that we cannot but feel a deep interest in the spiritual welfare and the future condition of those whose melodious strains are associated with some of our happiest hours at home or on the Sabbath, but whom we miss when we sing the Sacramental hymn. We think of them as hereafter recollecting the strains with which certain affecting words will forever be associated in their minds, and how they uttered protestations of love to Christ, petitions for pardon, hopes of heaven, contemplations of endless life, and the borrowed language of heaven in its ascriptions to God and to the Lamb. We are all familiar with that wonderful phenomenon of our natures, the memory of music; how a note or a chord, or a word, or a casual recollection, will cause a tune to sweep through the mind, preserving the unbroken order of its notes, though years have gone over us since it was last heard or sung; so that the singular saying of some philosophers that the vibrations of the air made by words sung or spoken, wander forever, seems to have a true counterpart within us, where the memories of music lie bound together, and to our recollections, with links of association more inseparable than words or places. Then what must it be for those to be lost, whose employment on earth has been to sing religious hymns, thereby identifying the most pathetic, the most thrilling truths, in correspondent expressions, with their future recollections of earth. May they remember these truths and these strains only with the redeemed, repeat them to themselves, and in our hearing, when faith and hope will enshrine love in her undivided empire over our hearts, and prayer shall have uttered its last Amen, and praise shall summon the minstrels of earth and heaven to their harps. Let it be impressed upon every one who assists in the public praises of God, that we must have a heart to sing the Sacramental hymn, on earth, before we can be included in the number of those harpers harping upon their harps.

"They sung a hymn." At the institution of an ordinance to commemorate the sufferings, the death of Jesus, they sung a hymn! he directing the service.

If a hymn could be appropriate then and there, if

Jesus, with Gethsemane and Calvary in view, led in singing a hymn, if he who took the cup and gave thanks joined in sacred praise before he went out to suffer, if the last act of worship which he performed with the disciples before the end came for which he was born, was, to sing, we are instructed and encouraged to turn every thing into praise, and in every thing by prayer and supplication, together with thanksgiving, to let our requests be made known unto God, and the peace of God which passeth all understanding shall keep our hearts and minds through Christ Jesus. In the midst of fiery trials, in the darkest hours, in the loneliest night-watches, even if we make our bed to swim with our tears, amid the fiercest opposition, in dangers, and even in the prospect of violent death, we have the example of Jesus teaching us with what composure and assurance we may remember that, in all these things, we are more than conquerors through him that loved us.

Words would fail to describe the themes for praise which are fit subjects for Sacramental Hymns. At the passover, that portion of the Psalms from the hundred and thirteenth, to the hundred and eighteenth inclusive, called by the Jews, *Hallel*, or Hallelujah Psalms, were sung by them; the first two previous to the feast, and the others at the conclusion. Whether these Psalms, or a special hymn, were sung at the institution of the Supper, we have no tradition. It is left to the varying circumstances of our times and conditions, to choose a hymn for each communion season, for how impossible it would be for one hymn to include the great themes which are appropriately made the burden of our songs at such times. We love to sing of the lost image of God restored by the free, unpurchased love of God, through the astonishing condescension of the Saviour; and the kind and gracious work of the ever blessed Spirit, whom we ought frequently to remember and praise, at the communion season, in connection with the Redeemer. Sometimes the distinction which has been made between fallen men and fallen angels, is the burden of our song; the particular application of divine mercy to each of our souls, so many at our side turning their faces away from this great salvation; the power of religion upon our hearts, to purify, elevate, cheer, ennoble, our whole being; the hopes it inspires, the joy it sets before us, and always and in connection with every thing else, the sufferings, the sorrow, the shame, the death of the Redeemer, and then his ascension and reign, his presence with us alway, and his second coming, our gathering together unto him,— what strains of music, and what words are competent to express these things? of which, nevertheless, it may be said to every true communicant, 'all are yours, and ye are Christ's and Christ is God's.'

Will there be a Sacramental Hymn at the marriage Supper of the Lamb? A principal expression of heavenly happiness is represented to be by singing and playing upon harps. We take that representation as conveying something as much like singing as heavenly things can be imaged by the earthly. Doubtless there will be a celebration, by acts of praise, of the finished work of Christ, and of the first grand assembly of the saints in heaven and of those who shall then come from the earth. If our Sacramental Hymns now make us feel and say that we never hear such singing elsewhere, let us expect that the hymn which will be the song of Moses and the Lamb, when passover, Lord's Supper, church-meeting, prayer, faith, hope, and singing itself, are each like a translated Enoch and Elijah, and from east and west, and north and south, as well the singers as the players on instruments shall be there, and every soul will have power to sing, its imperfect bodily structure being repaired and tuned, — let us expect, that the first choral song of heaven, that overture, that symphony, and then that burst of joy, at the marriage Supper of the Lamb, will be unlike any thing to which the morning stars have listened or that made the sons of God shout for joy. Of all the effects of sacred music on many of us, nothing surpasses that of the passage in the Messiah, " And his name shall be called Wonderful, Counsellor, the mighty God, the everlasting Father, the Prince of peace." But when the instruments of orchestras give place to harpers, with their hands waiting on their chords to sound out, at the signal, that " Wonderful, Counsellor, mighty God," and the uplifted cymbals of heaven make emphasis for those words, may each of us be there! each of us for whom this marriage Supper will have been provided, an invitation thereto, in the name of the bridegroom, having been given personally to every one who reads these lines.

Let us cease, therefore, to turn our backs, Sabbath after Sabbath, upon this Sacramental table. If we have no heart for the Sacramental hymn, we shall not, we cannot, join to celebrate the finished work of redemption. Christ died that each of us might sing, a redeemed, happy spirit, through the whole of our deathless being.

Angels have no sacramental hymn among their music. They could better perform the "Creation," and we the "Messiah," for of a sacramental hymn, as it may be called, it is said, and "no man could learn that song but the hundred and forty and four thousand which were redeemed from the earth." There is a bold expression in one of John Wesley's hymns: —

"By faith the upper choir we meet,
And challenge them to sing."

In vain would they emulate us in celebrating a recovery from sin and hell, in setting forth the experience of repentance, faith, hope, and all the spiritual affections of a renewed heart. It will be interesting for each of us to consider whether he could join in that "challenge," and bear his part in sustaining it. But what is this which comes to the mind in contrast with such proud eminence among the creatures of God? It is another "challenge" — and it is addressed to certain men by fallen angels — to the finally unconverted, and the false professors, of a Christian congregation. "They that carried us away captive required of us a song, and they that wasted us required of us mirth, saying, Sing us one of the songs of Zion." To what fearful exposures are we brought, O Christ, by this infinite love of thine, which, unless it succeeds to save us, will plunge us sevenfold deeper into hell.

"They went out into the Mount of Olives." There, for retirement and meditation, and for preparation, the little company retreated from their last passover, and from the first Lord's Supper. What became of that man whom the two disciples, by Christ's appointment, met, bearing a pitcher of water, and who showed them a large upper chamber furnished, where they made ready the passover? Jesus and his little company left his house, but did they leave him an alien from Christ, or was he his friend? Did he ever know, does he this day rejoice to know, the honor which came upon his house as the place of the last passover and its divine substitute? Or, does he mourn to think that the kingdom of God came nigh unto him, and that he knew not the time of his visitation? We naturally hope and believe that he was a friend of Christ, but at all events, the sacramental band left him and his dwelling, for the

Mount of Olives. The going out of the great company of the redeemed from their first meeting before the throne, families, circles of friends drawing off to their mansions, where shall we be, in that going out, after their great sacramental hymn, to their Mounts of Olives? There, no more to betray nor be betrayed, no more to weep, to suffer, to die, no more to be scattered, no more to labor with toil and pain, but everywhere and on all occasions finding living fountains of water, redemption having become a history, and the mediatorship having been resigned, and no more sacrifice for sin, shall each of us receive the end of his faith even the salvation of his soul? The Sacramental table now divides us. We part here; if we unite everywhere else, — at family prayers, at public worship — yet very many of us go asunder here, and so our feelings toward Christ will divide us in that day, when "terror and glory join in their extremes."

Another Sacramental table may never greet the eyes of some who read these lines. Ere it is spread again, what if they should spread for you that last, narrow bed, from which your eyes will be opened to see the Redeemer and his people leaving you, as here you leave them. It is not too late. To-day, the peaceful, touching sight, the table of the Lord, is to present itself to you, and you, lingering around that scene, can, by repenting and believing in Christ, be furnished by the hand of the Master himself, with the wedding garment. To-day, you not only may hear, but can join and sing, our Sacramental hymn, which, if you can sing with your heart, you may come to the table here, and be in the company of the Saviour's friends at his appearing and kingdom.

XII.

THE FIRST AND LAST EXODUS.

"Gather my saints together unto me; those that have made a covenant with me by sacrifice."

Six hundred thousand males, of twenty years old and upwards, together with women and children, marched forth from Egypt in a triumphal procession. "And the children of Israel went up harnessed out of the land of Egypt." A marginal note in the larger Bibles says, — "or, by five in a rank;" — not in tumultuary haste and confusion, as in fear, but in well-ordered ranks, they went forth. Not by small companies, set free at the death of a master, or their liberty purchased by one or two of their number, do they seek a sea-shore, waiting to be conveyed to some free land; nor are they private fugitives, begging their way to a place of freedom, but a nation is on the march, parents and children, chiefs and people, with their flocks and herds. In their coffers were the treasures of Egypt, which, by a sudden influence from the Almighty, their terrified lords and mistresses had heaped upon tnem, to hasten their flight. " He brought them forth also with silver and gold."

But perhaps this is the most wonderful of all: — " and there was not one feeble person among their tribes." Great God! we love and adore thee for this. Let us suppose that there had been some sick child, some lingering, dying husband, or wife, among the Hebrews, and the time came for the nation to take up its march. The nation must go, but one and another must stay, and languish and die, and others watch over dying beds, and bury their dead in a land made still more a house of bondage by the departure of their liberated nation. But it seems that in more than a million of people, there was " not one feeble person ;" — the only million of people, probably, in this world, of whom collectively, this had ever been true. In kind and gracious preparation of them for this deliverance, God had healed each one whom lingering illness, or a wound, or any infirmity had threatened to detain. No disabling accident near the time of departure, had been permitted to befall one of them. " Who is like unto thee, O people saved by the Lord, the shield of thy help, and who is the sword of thy excellency ? " " When Israel was a child then I loved him, and called my son out of Egypt."

Liberty achieved for them by mighty signs and wonders from the immediate hand of God, liberty obtained suddenly, unconditional, perpetual, excited this host, we may suppose, to the utmost pitch of human joy. Their music and banners, the glee and shouts of the young, the gratulations of families and friends, the noise of the camels, and flocks, and herds, the songs of praise bursting from the lips of the more impulsive, and awaking choruses on every side, the quick tramp of hoofs, the roar of wheels over those magnificent broad ways, with words of command and cheer from the subalterns of their great leader, exultations and laughter, ironical farewells at every obelisk and public work that reminded them of their brick without straw, and then an uproar of joy that they were to see those monuments of tyranny no more, — truly 'the shout of a king is among them,' and that exodus was a scene which, probably, will never be equalled but once in the history of the human race.

In one part of this triumphal host, there was something which, on many accounts, was as interesting as any thing in that great, moving spectacle. It was a sarcophagus, emblazoned with signs of royal honor, guarded with solemn pomp, and making, in some respect, in its appearance, a contrast to the general mirth; and yet a mellowed joy seems to be round about it, rather than sadness. It is "the bones of Joseph." "By faith Joseph when he died, made mention of the departure of the children of Israel, and gave commandment concerning his bones." "And Moses took the bones of Joseph with him; for he had straitly sworn the children of Israel, saying, God will surely visit you; and ye shall carry up my bones away hence with you." Dying amidst imperial honors, a grateful nation embalming his memory in their hearts, he would naturally have expected that, for all his father's house, his services would secure lasting favor and prosperity at the hands of the Egyptian kings. "Bold infidelity! turn pale and die!" For why, under such circumstances, did Joseph give such commandment concerning the removal of his bones, so honored and safe in the keeping of a nation which, under God, had been delivered by him from a seven years' famine? — Now, on their way out of Egypt to the yet unbuilt sepulchre in Shechem, these bones give impressive testimony to the faithfulness of God; they are themselves a sacramental symbol of faith, and, as such, must have had a powerful effect upon the leaders and the people in this eventful moment of their history.

Who are these people, and why are they here? These are the covenant people of God, the children of Abraham, his friend. They are on their way to a land selected from the whole habitable earth to be, for a long time, the home of the church, the land of Messiah, the scene of human redemption. This is the first stage of their journey to that land which is to be the glory of all lands, toward which the eyes of the world and the thoughts of heaven are to be turned for ages with surpassing interest.

Leaving them on their triumphal march, we will go back to Egypt, and look upon the former oppressors of Israel.

O fearful sight! we shrink back; we dare not go in.

Egypt is one house of mourning. All, all, are burying their dead. From Pharaoh's palace comes a funeral; the streets are filled with funerals, the air with wailings; the first-born child in every house is dead, the first-born of every fold and stall; thus while Israel marches forth with exultation, and God, their God, is with them, miserable Egypt is among the tombs, with their dead children. Had merely a child of every family died, the mortality might have seemed a mere epidemic; but that, in every case, the dead child should be the first-born, was a sign and wonder above their cavil. What curses were heaped upon Israel! How must they have been filled with rage at Israel's God! If the death of one child in a single family be an event of unsurpassed grief, the amount of sorrow in Egypt, where no house was without its dead, made good the declaration, — "none like it, nor shall be like it any more." Then they remember how they slew the male infants of Israel. God oftentimes makes men see their sin, again, in their punishment. In a word, great floods of sorrow, rolling and breaking over every house, mingled with rage, remorse, thoughts of vengeance, and shame at their defeat by this injured people and their God, make Egypt as great a contrast as possible to happy Israel, going forth from captivity to their destined home, with God for their guide and friend.

It was remarked, that probably there would never be but one event and scene in the history of the human race to be compared with this triumph of Israel and perdition of Egypt. There will be such an event, and such a scene, one in which every one of us will not only feel a personal interest, but bear a part.

We will take for a point of view a place from which we can see the righteous, raised from the dust of the earth and from the seas, at the moment when they are about to be caught up to meet the Lord in the air. From Abel, to the last surviving saints, they are on their way to heaven, together. Why on earth? Why have the redeemed left heaven? To receive the adoption, to wit, the redemption of their bodies. This resumption of the body is the finishing act of redemption. The departure of Israel is an emblem of the departure of the righteous from earth to heaven at the last day.

This is the people of God. They were given to Christ before the foundation of the world. That word is now accomplished: "And this is the Father's will that hath sent me, that of all which he hath given me, I should lose nothing; and I will raise it up at the last day." He planted a field and watered it, gathered out the stones thereof, set husbandmen to till it, and now, lo, the harvest of the earth is come, the sheaves are gathered and on their way to the garner.

Slowly, and one by one out of a family, and two out of a nation, for much of the time, was this people gathered, from every kindred and tongue, till now, a multitude which no man can number, they are the product of redemption, the result of an eternal plan, the fruit of unutterable pains and travail of soul on the part of their Redeemer and of his witnesses, and, in many cases, of themselves. God now possesses that for which alone he made the world and created man upon it; and with these He is to show to principalities and powers in heavenly places the manifold wisdom of God. Their history is to set forth more of God to the universe than all his works beside; and in the ages to come he will show the exceeding riches of his grace in his kindness toward them through Christ Jesus. "Happy art thou, O Israel; who is like unto thee, O people saved by the Lord, the shield of thy help, and who is the sword of thy excellency!"

They are delivered from the power of the enemy. While death and the grave held their bodies, their deliverance was not complete. Now the bars are broken, every precious treasure of a human form is yielded up, the last enemy is destroyed, which is death. Sin is, for them, forever put away, and its consequences; men and devils can no more afflict; going from earth, the righteous are going from the dominion of the god of this world. Farewell temptations, farewell vexations, farewell tribulations, an eternal farewell to every tear; the last chain is broken, the ransomed now "return, and come to Zion with songs and everlasting joy upon their heads; they shall obtain joy and gladness, and sorrow and sighing shall flee away."

They are on their way to a promised land. Land of promise, indeed! the metropolis of the universe; not a colony, not some undistinguished world, but the abode of God himself, the seat of his throne; a place prepared, exclusively, so far as we can infer from the Bible, for the habitation of angels and men. Infinite wisdom and skill selected and prepared that place; we should faint, more than Sheba's queen at Solomon's glory, if we should see it with bodily eyes. What a place, considered merely as a place, heaven must be, prepared by Infinite love and power for the abode of those who have been redeemed and saved at such cost. "For he hath prepared for them a city." Now, the meaning of those words begins to break upon us with new power, — "Father, I will that they whom thou hast given me be with me where I am, that they may behold my glory, which thou hast given me." He said, "I go to prepare a place for you, and if I go and prepare a place for you, I will come again and receive you unto myself; that where I am there ye may be also."

There will be a time when there will be very few, if

any, human beings in heaven; and where will its human inhabitants then be? At their graves, receiving each his glorified body. Then, what a return, and what a sight, when, reëntering heaven, the redeemed, with their forms like Christ's, approach the heavenly world with the Captain of their salvation at their head. O my soul, be among them! Advanced legions of angels blow with ten thousand trumpets, and begin to sing, "Lift up your heads, O ye gates, and be ye lifted up, ye everlasting doors; and the King of glory shall come in." The King of glory! never before did he receive that name with such accumulated honors upon it. Redeemer, thy glory now is full orbed. The joy of thy people is the joy of their Lord. O earth, it seems worth all thy travail, to have yielded such a scene as this. That one hour, that one scene, of reëntering heaven, of passing away from earth, with such spoils and triumph,— a lifetime of ecstasy is nothing compared with it; one might sit in chains threescore years, burn at the stake, be sawn asunder,— any thing would be a cheap purchase, for the joy of that hour. Recognitions, welcomes, fulness of joy, every sensibility touched with new sensations of pleasure, eternity in heaven before them, as they defile through those twelve gates, into the city,— the symbolical departure of Israel, glorious as it was, how can it be compared with this!

And now, the bones of Joseph, which were carried up out of Egypt by the triumphant church have found their antitype in the carrying away from earth, that house of bondage and place of graves, of a glorified body by every one who, as he fell asleep in Jesus, made mention, in his faith and hope, of this departing of the children of Israel. Not in a princely sarcophagus, but in a body like unto Christ's own glorious body, shall we each leave this Egypt, and (O in what an exalted sense!) be gathered to our fathers. "For I know that my Redeemer liveth, and that he shall stand at the latter day upon the earth; and though after my skin, worms destroy this body, yet in my flesh shall I see God: whom I shall see for myself, and mine eyes shall behold, and not another; though my reins be consumed within me."

But there is another part to this picture, as there was to the departure of Israel. There will be an Egypt at the last day; what is it? who will they be?

Unconverted men will be like Egypt to the departing church. They will be seen to be, like the Egyptians, the enemies of God. The signs and wonders of his providence and grace, public and personal, failed to make them repent. The messengers of God had no success with them, but every thing served only to harden their hearts. They would not join themselves to the covenanted Israel, they did not choose rather to suffer affliction with the people of God, than to enjoy the pleasures of sin for a season. But while mixed up with them on earth, the difference was not in all repects, so clearly made known. Every Communion Sabbath, it is true, brought forcibly to view a distinction between the church and the world, and disclosed this coming separation; but no public continued severance was made. "Let both grow together until the harvest, and in the time of harvest I will say to the reapers, Gather ye together first the tares, and bind them in bundles to burn them, but gather the wheat into my barn."

Impenitent men will be under the power of death. Having risen from their graves to meet the second death, and received their bodies to be more miserable in them, they are to spend eternity conversant only with that which is called in the Bible, Death, the loss, the perdition, of all good. And it will be a time of burial with them. They will bury every hope of reprieve, of mitigated pain, and every friend. The cry that went up from Egypt while Israel journeyed away, would be drowned in that last weeping and wailing.

Impenitent men will be undergoing punishment. Forward they must move to the left hand of Christ, to be judged and sentenced. What a hideous throng! What a contrast to the righteous! The good are gathered out; not a solitary good man, no little one, is in that multitude, but every one is wicked, under arrest, suffering punishment already, and expecting more. There are the sinners of the old world, and of Sodom and Gomorrah, liars, thieves, tyrants, murderers, the unclean, the profane; while the more reputable and outwardly respectable of the enemies of Christ will be mixed up promiscuously with them. A man, hitherto respectable and respected, on committing some offence against society for which secret wickedness had prepared him, is sent to the State prison, and while they are putting on him the twain colored dress, he says, This is worse than all. Must I march with locked step and folded arms in a file with convicts? Perhaps he was a graduate of a college, perhaps he preached, perhaps he held a high place in the Christian church. Justice makes no account of our standing, or past associations, nor considers our refinement; down we go to the common herd of the vile, if we turn aside to crooked ways, and are led forth with the workers of iniquity. As though they were a chain-gang, all the finally impenitent will go to their final doom. Old companions in sin, members of the same impenitent families, people who had only heard of each other, such as distinguished conquerors, wicked sovereigns and popes, murderers, knaves, whose names are on the annals of crime, will meet, and their meeting will be with revulsion and hatred. The sight of the righteous passing away will be the aggravation of their misery. Their personal separations and grief will be the most dreadful. 'O my father! mother! my husband! my wife! my child! my brother! my sister! Once I sat by your side, and heard the same gospel; hundreds of times I left your side, and went from the Lord's table where so affectionately and with tears I was urged to come, and where I should have been as welcome as you. But month after month for years, I went away from Christ; now, Christ and heaven are going away from me. One more opportunity to accept Christ! to profess him before men! to join the company of those who showed his death until he come! He is come! All is lost! Once the many who, with me, left the communion table behind, countenanced me; now, this great multitude of them affrights me!' — But cries and regrets are vain. All this is the beginning of sorrows.

Thus, while the Israel of God will go from earth and enter heaven with joy, impenitent men will be as Egypt was while burying her dead, except that every one will himself be a mourner over his own soul irrecoverably lost. Should they attempt to follow after the righteous, they could not reach them. They have loaded them with their wishes and their envyings at their lot, and they have departed; all the happiness which they ever had in common, the righteous have carried away with them, and the wicked are spoiled of every thing. The prophecies of the New Testament are now fulfilled like the prophecies of the Old; the thirteenth chapter of Matthew, with its parables of the field, and the net, is fulfilled, and, with the twenty-fifth chapter of Matthew, has ceased to be prediction, and is now history.

It was 'on the morrow after the passover,' that 'the children of Israel went out with an high hand in the sight of all the Egyptians.' The night before, every head of a house among them killed a lamb, went to the door, dipped the hyssop in the bowl of blood, and struck the door-posts, and the lintel overhead, with the dripping herb. That saved him and his house. "By faith he kept the passover and the sprinkling of blood, lest he that destroyed the first-born should touch them." As we look now, once more, on that great throng who are passing away from earth and entering heaven, we may consider that, leaving out of the case those who went to heaven in tender years, every one of the redeemed had feelings which qualified him to partake of the Lord's Supper.

We must have them, or we see what will happen. The feelings which qualify us for admission to heaven and to the Lord's table are substantially the same. If I have believed in Christ as my passover slain for me, and his blood has been my plea, and is my defence, I belong to the invisible church; and one proof of this will be, I shall seek his fold. "Tell me, O thou whom my soul loveth, where thou feedest, and where thou makest thy flock to rest at noon." As surely as we continue to divide here at the table of Christ, we shall divide at the last day, and the same thing which divides us here will divide us there, and that is, our feelings toward Christ, and our relation to him.

As we see Israel coming out of Egypt under the protection and by the special hand of God, we mourn to remember that multitudes of that rejoicing people failed to reach Canaan. It is not enough to leave Egypt; it is not enough to be numbered with the people of God. "I will therefore put you in remembrance, though ye once knew this, how that the Lord, having saved the people out of the land of Egypt, afterward destroyed them that believed not." No tokens of divine favor, no privileges, no high standing among the people of God, give us any exemption from punishment, if we wilfully sin. There is no favoritism with God toward the most distinguished of his servants, if they commit iniquity. For, "he spared not the angels which sinned, but cast them down to hell, and delivered them into chains of darkness to be reserved unto judgment." We serve a jealous God. If we make Christ a minister of sin, by continuing in sin that grace may abound, all his unutterable work of suffering and death will be a stone to fall upon us; we shall go from the Lord's table and from Communion Sabbaths to a deeper, a far more intolerable, place in misery and despair even than those who sinned in heaven.

"Let us therefore fear, lest a promise being left us of entering into his rest, any of you should seem to come short of it."

Every Communion Sabbath leaves the number of our Sacramental seasons less; they will soon end; let us redeem the time, — and make full proof of the influence which the ordinance of the Supper was designed to have upon us.

Perhaps the approaching Communion Sabbath is the last for another year, and you are not yet a Christian. Mourn, ye wasted months; this immortal soul is yet without hope, and without God in the world. When the anniversary of this Sabbath returns, the past furnishes no ground for assured hope that he will have come to Christ; he is venturing into the perilous future with no covenanted protection against eternal death. From the Lord's table, and from the most special appeal which Christ makes to us, he has turned away as many times, the past year, as Christ has said from that table, "This do in remembrance of me."

"To him that is joined to all the living there is hope." "And yet there is room." "The Spirit and the bride say, Come." "As the Holy Ghost saith, To-day, if ye will hear his voice, harden not your hearts."

XIII.

EXPOSTULATION.

"AND NOW IF YE WILL DEAL KINDLY AND TRULY WITH MY MASTER, TELL ME; AND IF NOT, TELL ME; THAT I MAY TURN TO THE RIGHT HAND OR TO THE LEFT."

WHY DO YOU NOT COME TO THE LORD'S SUPPER?

Answer 1. "Christians do not appear to me to be better people than many others who are not communicants."

The answer, in a more extended form, includes such remarks as these: 'I am acquainted with many who are equal to any professing Christians, but they do not consider it necessary to join a church. I see people remain at the Lord's table who do things which I would scorn to do; some of them I know to be wholly unfit to partake of that sacred ordinance.'

We will allow that every communicant has a superior in moral character out of the church; nay, that all who commune, are unfit to partake.

Christ died for you, nevertheless; to you he speaks from his table: "This do in remembrance of me." For Paul received a special revelation from Christ with regard to the Supper, (see 1 Cor. xi. 23–26,) and tells us that this ordinance is appointed by Christ to be observed "until he come." So that let others be unworthy, you, if you believe in the Christian religion, must admit that the duty is incumbent on you, as an act of gratitude to the Lord Jesus your Saviour, to comply with his requirement and show forth his death.

With such a correct, and even high moral standard as you manifestly profess, it is peculiarly obligatory on you, especially with the light afforded you with respect to exemplary conduct, to be a professing Christian. These people whom you reflect upon, perhaps are not so well instructed as you are, or so highly furnished with a nice discernment of right and wrong. How useful a Christian you would be with your high standard and sense of propriety, should you be a follower of Christ.

But are you aware that, if it be right for you to turn your back upon a whole church, for the sins of a few, it would be right for all to forsake the Lord's Supper, on the ground that some, or many, communicants are not as they should be?

You profess to esteem some who are not communicants, and who decline to be, as highly as professing Christians. By the solemn hour of death, tell me, Are there not professing Christians whose place, on a dying bed, you would rather take, than that of any friend of yours out of the church of Christ?

Would you not go to his judgment-seat from his table with a special feeling of safety and peace?

Suppose that your parent should make a dying request that, on the first Saturday evening of every month, or the last Saturday evening of every second month, you and the other children should together read a letter of his or hers, or look upon an appointed keepsake? If you were a kind and dutiful child, it would make no difference with you whether one and another proved unworthy or neglectful as a child. You would use the memorial with the greater zeal, and mourn that any one could so forget himself and his deceased parent as to neglect it. If you ever prayed, that memorial would be the means of making you pray most earnestly for the recreant member of the family.

"Every one of us shall give account of himself to God." Christ said of the straight gate and narrow way, — "and few there be that find it." Many shall say, 'Lord, Lord,' to whom he will say, I never knew you. Let it be that the larger portion of every church will be of this description; you have a soul to save, a God to serve, a Saviour to love; for Christ died for you.

Answer 2. "I do not think it necessary to salvation, that one should join the church."

It is necessary, in order to be saved, to have feelings toward Christ which will make you desire to be at his table.

If you believe in Christ, you will be grateful to him, and you will wish to show it, by complying with his most reasonable and affecting requirement. If you have no desire to be at the table of Christ, you have no such feelings toward him as are necessary in order to be saved.

Answer 3. "If I make a profession of religion, I make promises which I can never keep."

No such promise is ever required or made. The engagement is never unconditional in making a profession of religion; but it is coupled with an expression of dependence on God; and we promise that, with his aid, we will endeavor to walk in all godliness and honesty. Every one fails to reach even his own standard; in many things we offend, in all we come short, and daily need repentance and atoning blood.

But in other things, we never hesitate to promise where our feelings are deeply interested; we do not then take counsel of our fears, and refuse to do the best we can because of expected failure to be perfect.

When we make a profession, we do not say, Behold, I am perfect, but, Behold, I am vile. I am a lost, perishing sinner, unless Christ shall save me. My heart is depraved, I am prone to sin; but I repent; I look to Christ for pardon; I wish to live a religious life; without the aid of the Holy Spirit, I can do nothing. I profess to have had a change of heart; to love holiness, to hate sin; my life is to be a conflict between good and evil; but I wish to live for him who died for me, to deny myself, and take up the cross and follow him.

Answer 4. "I am not worthy."

Should you ever profess to be worthy, it would, probably, be best for you to wait longer.

If you feel yourself to be a sinner, this is an essential qualification. If you have no expectation of being saved but through the sacrifice of Christ, that is another. If you commit your soul to him, if you ever have any thing like covenant transactions with him in prayer, you have believed in Christ.

Should a dear friend come to you in distress on account of sin, or if you were at the dying bed of one who should ask, What must I do to be saved, do you think, do you hope, that you would be able to direct that soul to Christ? The common difficulties and objections of such persons, would you, probably, be able to meet, out of your own experience? If you could, why not take the comfort of that faith and hope with which you would thus seek to inspire him?

Answer 5. "My companion, or intimate friend, is not inclined to make a profession of religion, and if I do it, I shall make a separation between us."

Your companion and you, dear friend, have each a a soul to save, or lose. You wish to lead a quiet, comfortable life together, undisturbed by such a difference of feelings and conduct as a profession of religion by one of you, without the other, would occasion. This life is a handbreadth. It is a probationary state for eternity; now, what if your companion should reproach you hereafter, and say, You knew the truth, and your duty; had you been decided, I should have followed you; or if not, you would, at least, have saved your soul, and perhaps the souls of the children. You made me happy, in many things, but you were false, you were cruel, to my eternal interests.

To do our duty in this thing is the surest way to encourage others. Unless there be a good prospect that a companion, or friend, will, erelong, make a profession of religion, and thus both have the pleasure of doing it together, it is wrong as well as hazardous, and also injurious to the spiritual interests of the friend, to delay. We must also remember who has said, "He that loveth father or mother more than me, is not worthy of me."

Few things are more disastrous than to trifle with, or neglect, our Christian hope. By failing to do our duty at a proper time, we are liable to be confused as to the evidences of personal religion, we begin to doubt and fear, and thus many spend years in darkness and sorrow.

These remarks are not made with a view to urge any to take so important a step as the one in question, prematurely. But there is an extreme which is opposite to precipitancy. Christ says, "Follow me." Each one should seek direction, and while no man can take from us, nor share, the responsibility of such a step, we may receive great assistance by stating our difficulties and obtaining advice.

But the time is short. "Whosoever shall confess me before men, him shall the Son of Man also confess before the angels of God." To confess Christ is not, indeed, one disconnected act; our life must confess Christ; that confession of him, however, must have a beginning, and it is evinced in proposing to join ourselves to the visible church. When we stand before him and render up our account, is our reason for not coming to his table such, that we shall be able to present it to him, with any confidence that it will be accepted? and, in view of it will he probably waive our obligation to have been his follower, and say, "Enter thou into the joy of thy Lord!"

Or, do we apprehend that his reply would be, "He that denieth me before men, shall be denied before the angels of God?"

That you now seriously lay these things to heart, "I give thee charge in the sight of God, who quickeneth all things, and before Christ Jesus, who, before Pontius Pilate witnessed a good confession." When, for your sake, he went to the judgment-hall, remember that he himself furnished the only ground upon which they could condemn him; that they sought witnesses, and found none; that at last two false witnesses appeared, but that "neither so did their witness agree together," and that then, before the High-Priest, and before Pontius Pilate, Jesus made a profession and a confession, on which alone they were able to crucify him.

He knew this, and there, for your sake, he "witnessed a good confession."

"Let us go forth, therefore, unto him without the camp, bearing his reproach."

How does our finding fault with Christians, our plea that we can be saved without coming to the Lord's table, that we shall not live up to our engagement, that our friends will not like it, or that we are not worthy, and all the various excuses which we plead against a Christian profession, appear, when we compare them with what he did for us? Who that has a heart which is ever touched by gratitude and love, can contemplate his Saviour, suffering and dying for him, and not at once give himself away to him, resolved, if he must perish, to perish endeavoring to serve this Saviour and Friend!

Answer 6. When all other objections have been answered, it is common to hear it said, "I must be far better than I am before I take so solemn a step. Sometimes I persuade myself that I am a Christian; but this is transient, for soon I feel strangely indifferent to spiritual duties. I do not always enjoy prayer as I ought. I frequently take up some interesting book when, perhaps, I should take the Bible. I have not an entire control of my temper, as I should have were I a

Christian. I am not good enough to be a member of the church."

It is remarkable that, while with regard to our conduct we look wholly to the righteousness of Christ, yet as it regards our feelings we look for perfection, or to the law of God, to be justified and accepted. So that we present the singular spectacle of trusting in Christ alone to justify us, as to our conduct, but seek to have our emotions, our religious experience, entirely right, to make them acceptable with God.

But if by feeling as we ought, we may obtain a ground of justification, we may also do without Christ in every other respect.

We cannot be justified through conformity to the law of God, neither in our conduct, nor in our feelings; "for the law made nothing perfect, but the bringing in of a better hope did, by the which we draw nigh unto God." Even the faith which saves us has no merit, any more than the stretching forth of the beggar's hand entitles him to the alms which he receives.

"But still," it is replied, "our feelings are evidences of our being born of the Spirit."

Our capability of certain feelings is essential evidence; their strength, their uniformity, vary in different cases. Have you at any time loved God? Have you committed your soul to Christ for pardon and salvation? Have you loved holiness for its own sake, and been sorry for sin as committed against God? Do not reply, " Not so much as I ought." Have you ever been capable of one or more of these things? If an infant has breathed, it has lived; if you have at any time been capable of one spiritual affection, you have been born of the Spirit.

For such as you, Christ has appointed his Church, with its ordinances. The good Shepherd has folds, and provision in them and in his pastures adjacent. You must not wait for a vigorous growth in the wilderness before you enter the sheepfold.

" But what if I should lose my present evidence, poor as it is, of being a Christian, after joining the Church? How deplorable it must be to find one's self in an unregenerate state after joining the Church!"

Even if this should prove to be the case with you notwithstanding you endeavored to act sincerely, you must not despair. You did not act presumptuously. The way to be saved will be the same as now; instead of renouncing your Christian profession, you will need to do only that which the gospel now requires.

It will not be strange if, after joining the church, your evidence of being a Christian will seem to you less than before. The candle which was but just lighted and set in your heart, disclosed at first but a little of your moral deformity; but when its flame is stronger and brighter, you may begin to be dismayed at further disclosures. Not that you will be worse than before, but you will see yourself more distinctly, the more you know of God, and so you will increasingly abhor yourself. This will be a hopeful sign. If your desire and endeavor still is to be a Christian, know, that right desires are among the best evidences of piety. Not one of the beatitudes in the Sermon on the Mount applies to religious confidence and joy; they all pertain to states of mind nearly related to humility and contrition. Look away from yourself; cease to estimate your frames of mind as to their value, for in themselves they are, at best, like all our righteousnesses; but there is a perfect righteousness provided for us in Christ, and our exercises of mind are useful chiefly as they testify that we seek to be found in him, not having our own righteousness.

Before another communion Sabbath arrives, be persuaded to go to your pastor, or to some Christian friend, and disclose your feelings; take counsel, follow good advice. Agree now that you will do this. Say, "I will go in the strength of the Lord God; I will make mention of thy righteousness, even of thine only."

In our intercourse with God we must not be dilatory. In business, and even in complimentary affairs, it is not excused.

Read and ponder the truth contained in the closing part of these words, from Bunyan's description of the Wicket Gate:—

"So in process of time Christian got up to the gate.

Now over the gate there was written, 'Knock, and it shall be opened unto you.'

"He knocked, therefore, more than once or twice, saying:—

> May I now enter here? Will he within
> Open to sorry me, though I have been
> An undeserving rebel? Then shall I
> Not fail to sing his lasting praise on high.'

"At last there came a grave person to the gate, named Good-will, who asked who was there? and whence he came? and what he would have?

"CHRISTIAN. Here is a poor burdened sinner. I come from the city of Destruction, but am going to Mount Zion, that I may be delivered from the wrath to come. I would therefore, Sir, since I am informed that by this gate is the way thither, know if you are willing to let me in?

"'I am willing, with all my heart,' said he; and with that he opened the gate.

"So when Christian was stepping in, the other gave him a pull. Then said Christian, 'What means that?' The other told him, 'A little distance from this gate, there is erected a strong castle, of which Beelzebub is the captain; from thence, both he and they that are with him shoot arrows at those that come up to this gate, if haply they may die before they can enter in.'"

Let us briefly review the topics of this book.

CHRIST DIED FOR US. That which we chiefly dread, he endured, for every one of us, that we might be saved.

ONE SACRIFICE FOR SINS, attested by all the ancient sacrifices, and fulfilling their design as representatives of his atoning death, stands waiting to justify him that believeth in Jesus.

MIRACLES AT THE CRUCIFIXION leave no room to question the divine authority of the Sufferer, or the stupendous import of his sacrifice, who himself bare our sins in his own body on the tree.

THE THREE CROSSES teach us the relation which we and the sinful, tempting world should hold to Christ, in view of his own death upon the cross, where "he gave himself for our sins, that he might deliver us from this present evil world, according to the will of God and our Father."

MEMBERSHIP IN CHRIST, to which he admits us, is set forth to us by saying to every believing sinner, "For we are members of his body, of his flesh, and of his bones."

"HE SHOWED THEM HIS HANDS AND HIS FEET," to convince and persuade his unbelieving friends that it was he who died for them and rose again. We too may, almost, say, — "We have heard, we have seen with our eyes, we have looked upon, our hands have handled, — the word of life."

COMMUNION WITH CHRIST at his table, is the great

object for which it is spread; this communion is the privilege of all who by faith have fellowship with their Saviour.

SALUTATIONS AT THE SEPULCHRE between our risen Lord and one who had been a great sinner, have shown us the tenderness, the intimacy, of his love to those who love him, and the near approach to him, by faith and love, which they may enjoy.

THE WALK TO EMMAUS, still further shows us the condescending regard of Christ for the individuals of his people, and how easy it is for him to resolve the doubts and confirm the faith of all who truly seek him.

THOU PREPAREST A TABLE BEFORE ME, and such a table! meeting all my wants, and convincing me of the height and depth and length and breadth of a love which passeth knowledge.

THE SACRAMENTAL HYMN raises "the heavenward flame," cheering us to pursue the Christian life and to expect an eternity of praise among the ransomed with their harps and songs.

THE FIRST AND LAST EXODUS of the church of God,—leaving a guilty world,—their enemies and the enemies of God, admonish us that there will, as now, be only friends and enemies of Christ,—wheat and tares, in the field,—good and bad, in the net, in the end of the world; that we, at this moment, belong, each of us, to one or the other, of these great divisions, and that our present feelings toward Christ need but to be confirmed, and our condition for eternity is determined beyond the possibility of change.

"THEN SAID HE UNTO HIM, A CERTAIN MAN MADE A GREAT SUPPER AND BADE MANY;

"AND SENT HIS SERVANT AT SUPPER TIME TO SAY TO THEM THAT WERE BIDDEN, COME; FOR ALL THINGS ARE NOW READY. . . . . AND THE SERVANT SAID, LORD, IT IS DONE, AS THOU HAST COMMANDED, AND YET THERE IS ROOM."

THE END.

www.ingramcontent.com/pod-product-compliance
Lightning Source LLC
LaVergne TN
LVHW011208110826
845150LV00006B/1361

* 9 7 8 1 4 2 5 5 1 8 3 3 2 *